God of Love and God of Judgment

God of Love and God of Judgment

STEPHEN K. MORONEY

WIPF & STOCK · Eugene, Oregon

GOD OF LOVE AND GOD OF JUDGMENT

Wipf & Stock
A division of Wipf and Stock Publishers
199 W. 8th Ave., Suite 3
Eugene, OR 97401

www.wipfandstock.com

ISBN 13: 978-1-60608-897-5

Manufactured in the U.S.A.

Contents

Preface

PICTURES OF GOD

Some people picture God as an indulgent grandparent with an all-accepting smile. In their minds, God supports whatever we do and never judges anyone for anything. Other people picture God as a police officer with a radar gun set to record all our failures. In their minds, God detests us for our sins and looks forward to doling out the punishment we deserve. Both of these pictures of God ("love without judgment" and "judgment without love") are seriously flawed, but over the centuries many people have gravitated toward these mistaken extremes. This book takes up the challenge (and it is a challenge!) of trying to understand how a God of love can also be a God of judgment.

HOW THE BOOK GOT STARTED

I became interested in the subject of judgment through reading the Bible. Several issues did not make sense to me. *Who* does the judging: God the Father, God the Son, or God's people?[1] *What* is going to be judged: our faith in Jesus or our works?[2] *Why* does God render such varying judgments—allowing Cain to live when he murders his brother, but killing Uzzah on the spot when he tries to keep the Ark of the Covenant from tipping over?[3] *How* do we obey Jesus' command *to not judge* others and

---

1. On God the Father judging, see Matthew 10:28 and John 8:50. On God the Son judging, see Acts 10:42 and 2 Timothy 4:1. On God's people judging, see Matthew 19:28 and 1 Corinthians 6:3.

2. On our faith in Jesus, see Matthew 10:32–33; John 3:16–18, 3:36; Romans 4:1–6; and Ephesians 2:8–9. On our works, see Matthew 16:24–27, 25:31–46; Romans 2:5–8; 2 Corinthians 5:10; and Revelation 20:12–13.

3. Genesis 4:8–16 and 2 Samuel 6:6–8 (paralleled in 1 Chronicles 13:9–11).

also Paul's command *to judge* those within the church?[4] These questions drove me to dig deeper into Scripture.

My first step was to read through *The One Year Bible*, which arranges Scripture into 365 daily readings. Every time I spotted a reference to judgment, I made a note in the margin. It turned out to be a lot of notes. I encountered some aspect of judgment in the readings for 352 days out of the year—over ninety-five percent.[5] I found references to judgment in sixty-three of the sixty-six books of the Bible—also over ninety-five percent.[6] I had always known it was there, but I was stunned that judgment was such a dominant theme.

Next I wanted to see what other authors had to say about the topic. I found many books on the "end times" (the rapture, tribulation, and hell). But to my knowledge, it has been a couple of generations since anyone has written a book specifically on what the whole Bible teaches about judgment.[7] So, I was more persuaded than ever that we need a twenty-first-century book on what the Christian Scriptures have to say about judgment.

I became all the more convinced when I perused the shelves of our local Christian bookstore. Here I came across lots of books on grace, forgiveness, and healing—many of them fine, uplifting works—but hardly a

---

4. Matthew 7:1–5 and 1 Corinthians 5:1–12.

5. The only days I found with no mention of judgment were February 13, 23; May 29; June 6, 8; July 9, 20, 21; August 20, 21, 24; September 7; and December 1. Every other day addresses some aspect of the topic. Since the *One Year Bible* repeats the Psalms twice, I included references to judgment (and love in note 8 below) in the Psalms only the first time they appeared, during the first half of the year, to avoid double counting.

6. Here I follow the Protestant canon, though judgment also appears in what are sometimes called the books of the Apocrypha—which are included in Catholic and Orthodox Bibles. The three books with no obvious, overt references to judgment are Song of Songs, Philemon, and 3 John.

7. Recent publications on judgment with which I interact in this book include Steven J. Keillor, *God's Judgments* and Dan O. Via, *Divine Justice, Divine Judgment*. The most recent attempt to summarize what the whole Bible teaches on this subject is Leon Morris, *The Biblical Doctrine of Judgment*. This is a wonderful scholarly work, especially in its word studies, but it has long been out of print, is just sixty-five pages in length, and treats God's judgment apart from God's love. On the topic of retributive reward and punishment, see Stephen H. Travis, *Christ and the Judgement of God*. Technical scholarly books include Marius Reiser, *Jesus and Judgment*; Steven Bryan, *Jesus and Israel's Traditions of Judgment and Restoration*; and Chris VanLandingham, *Judgment & Justification in Early Judaism and the Apostle Paul*. Themes of God's just judgment and merciful love are also treated on a more popular level in David Clotfelter, *Sinners in the Hands of a Good God*.

word on judgment could be found. Most Christians are acquainted with the bright promise to Judah in Jeremiah 29:11—"'For I know the plans I have for you,' declares the Lord, 'plans to prosper you and not to harm you, plans to give you a hope and a future.'" We are less familiar with the Lord's gloomier promise to Jerusalem in Jeremiah 21:10—"I have determined to do this city harm and not good." We do not make posters or jewelry emblazoned with Jeremiah 44:27—"For I am watching over them for harm, not for good." After conducting my research, I was sure that a book on judgment would benefit twenty-first-century readers by reacquainting them with what the Bible teaches on this vital subject.

HOW THE BOOK CHANGED

So, a few years ago I composed a full manuscript—a fat pile of pages devoted to what the Bible says about judgment. But there were two problems with it. First, it was depressing. I did not even want to read it. Who else would? Then again, I told myself, sometimes the truth is depressing, but ultimately it is still good for us. A lot of what the prophets had to say was depressing initially. Bad news from a doctor can be the kick in the pants that we need to change our poor health habits. I tried to convince myself that a book on judgment was the hard theological medicine we need, especially today.

But I could not bring myself to publish the manuscript because of a second problem. When I really stepped back and thought about it, I did not believe in my approach. Originally my thinking had been: "Many authors have written about God's grace, love, and mercy. I will fill in the missing gaps by writing a book about God's judgment, justice, and wrath." The problem was my manuscript was just as one-sided as the others—the only difference being that mine focused on the "dark" side. A book about God's judgment that does not include God's love is just as lacking as a book about God's love that does not include God's judgment. What is really needed is a book about both.

So, again I read the Bible cover-to-cover, this time taking notes every time I came across the subject of love—a much cheerier task! Once more I found myself taking a lot of notes. Some aspect of love appeared in the readings for 336 days of the year (over ninety-two percent).[8] I found

---

8. The only days I found with no mention of love were March 3, 6, 7; April 8, 14, 26; June 6, 10, 15, 17, 19; July 4, 5, 6, 7; August 7, 10, 12, 16, 18, 22, 29; September 10; November 1, 12, 13; and December 13, 18, 29. Every other day addresses some aspect of the topic.

references to love in sixty-three of the sixty-six books of the Bible (over ninety-five percent).[9] There is no getting around it—love and judgment are both major themes in Scripture. When we focus on one theme without the other, we fall into all sorts of problems.

Sadly, those problems appear again and again in the pages of church history and in modern life. Many people have a one-sided view of God as only judgment or only love. In response to these recurring problems, I propose a solution that sounds simple but is challenging to achieve—developing a theology that joins love and judgment together.

The book is divided into three parts, each of which contains two chapters. Part one (the first two chapters) explores misunderstandings of God's judgment. Part two (the middle two chapters) focuses on misunderstandings of God's love. Part three (the final two chapters) tries to avoid these problems by joining love and judgment together in our understanding of God and in our own lives. Ultimately, this book makes the case that the God of love and God of judgment are not two different "Gods" or two "faces of God" that are irreconcilable. Rather, love and judgment are joined together in the perfect union of God's indivisible character. The God revealed in the Christian Scriptures is both a God of love and God of judgment.

TIPS ON USING THE BOOK

Most readers will be interested only in the main text of the book, and they should feel free to ignore the footnotes. The notes are intended for students, ministers, scholars, and others who are curious about the research details and want to follow up on the sources listed in the bibliography. Some people will want to discuss this book with others in a home study, church class, or formal academic course. To help groups get the conversation started, questions for reflection and discussion are included at the end of each chapter.

How can a God of love also be a God of judgment? If God loves everyone, what is the point of judgment? Is there any way for us to know how God is judging today? These are not just daunting issues for theologians to ponder. They are urgent questions for everyone. Our answers

---

9. The three books with no obvious, overt references to love are Esther, Obadiah, and Habakkuk, though it could be argued that love is implicitly present in each of these books—moving the total toward one hundred percent.

can profoundly affect our relationships with God and with each other. Coming to grips with these issues is a vital part of our spiritual journeys. In chapter one, we begin the journey with a terrifying phone call my wife received recently, something that no parent ever expects to hear.

ACKNOWLEDGMENTS

I WOULD LIKE TO thank several colleagues and relatives for their suggestions and encouragement during the production of this book. Special thanks go to Janice Anderson, Geoff Bowden, Jay Case, David Entwistle, Bryan Hollon, Michael Howell-Moroney, Greg Linville, Mike McGowan, John Moroney, Joy Moroney, Grace Moroney, Margaret Moroney, Sue Moroney, Suzanne Nicholson, Nate Phinney, Greg Roberts, Scott Waalkes, Karen Warner, Sunday school classes at Faith Bible Church, and my Spring 2009 Contemporary Theology class at Malone University. Thanks also to Malone University for supporting the writing of this book through provision of a sabbatical leave during the spring term of 2008.

PART ONE

Judgment without Love

Thus Judgeth the Lord

Perils of Proclaiming God's Judgment in Current Events

GOD'S JUDGMENT AND CATASTROPHES

TWO WEEKS AGO (AS I write) we received a terrifying phone call from our older daughter, Grace, who was in the middle of a tornado—literally! She was calling while holding a pillow over her head and crouching with her roommate in the bathtub of their college dorm room at Union University (Tennessee). As my wife listened on her cell phone, the tornado ripped through the campus—blowing some of Grace's friends out of their bathtubs, causing an estimated 40 million dollars in damage, and destroying approximately 70 percent of student housing. There were many serious injuries but no fatalities on campus. The university president stated publicly: "God providentially protected the lives of our students." Some of the students, however, thought God might have sent the tornado to shake them out of their spiritual complacency and make them more serious about putting God first in their lives. A few even wondered quietly if the tornado might have been God's hand of judgment.

Others do not wonder quietly to themselves but proclaim loudly in public that God's hand of judgment is upon us. It happens every year or two. An earthquake strikes California and hundreds of websites shout that the seismic activity is clearly God's judgment since its epicenter was near the hub of video pornography production. A hurricane hits the Gulf Coast and religious figures declare it is God's judgment against gambling and other sinful practices in the area. Some say the most costly natural disaster in U.S. history, Hurricane Katrina, was God's judgment on the depravity of New Orleans. Such pronouncements raise a question that people have grappled with for centuries: can we discern God's judgment in the events of history and the events of our times?

Many Puritans believed we could. They often saw God meting out judgment in the terrible happenings of their day. What are usually considered natural disasters to us (droughts, earthquakes, and floods) were plainly signs of God's wrath against sin, in the minds of many Puritans. Likewise, what we usually think of as personal misfortunes (financial ruin, serious illness, or "premature death") were often believed by Puritans to be instances of God's judgments. When something bad happened, the obvious explanation was that God was sending heavenly judgment for earthly sin.

In contrast to most Americans today (see chapter three), the Puritans had a strong sense of God as judge—an image often impressed on them from the pulpit. It has been estimated that in the course of a lifetime, the typical Puritan heard approximately 7,000 sermons totaling 10,000 hours of preaching. Those who began to nod off to sleep were prodded awake by parents or deacons! Many of the sermons spoke of God's deep love, but others thundered God's judgment. Just reading some of the sermon titles gives us a sense for their direct preaching on judgment. At the turn of the seventeenth century, published sermons included *The Great Day of Judgment* (Samuel Lee, 1692); *Impenitent Sinners Warned of Their Misery and Summoned to Judgment* (Samuel Willard, 1698); *The Vain Youth Summoned to Appear at Christ's Bar* (Samuel Moody, 1707); and *Persuasions from the Terror of the Lord* (Cotton Mather, 1711). Only a few decades later, Jonathan Edwards preached his famous sermon, *Sinners in the Hands of an Angry God* (1741).

TRACING THE FINGER OF GOD IN THOMAS BEARD'S *THEATRE OF GOD'S JUDGMENTS*

Aside from the sermons they heard, many Puritans were also influenced by stories they read in Thomas Beard's renowned book, *The Theatre of God's Judgments*. First published in 1597, the book was reissued, revised, and expanded over the years.[1] By the time it was published in abbreviated form in 1786, Puritan experts say that Beard's work "had indisputably be-

---

1. In this chapter I cite the 1631 printing, updated occasionally for modern spelling and grammar.

come a popular classic," and it represented "the most widely popularized and commonly accepted Puritan view of providence."[2]

According to this Puritan view of providence, God directs human affairs in such a way that "nothing in the world comes to pass by chance," but rather "only and always by the prescription of his will." Historical events show us how God rewards virtue and punishes vice. In this framework, punishment "follows sin as a shadow does the body." So, when we read both "biblical history" and "secular history," Beard said, we should diligently "mark the effects of God's providence and of his justice."[3] As Beard traced the finger of God's providence in history, the main lesson was that God judges sinners.

Beard's book is basically a compilation of stories about what happened to people who broke the Ten Commandments. Nearly every section begins with biblical narratives of God's judgments and then moves seamlessly into post-biblical history. Beard stated boldly that "there was never any that set themselves against the Church of God, but God set himself against them by some notable judgment."[4] Very often, in Beard's stories, God's punishment was tailored specifically to the perpetrator's sin.

Thomas Arondel, who prohibited ministers from speaking the word of God, "had his own tongue so swollen that it stopped his own mouth"—leading to death by starvation. An official named Felix swore "he would ride up to his spurs in the blood of Lutherans," but that night, "the hand of God so struck him, that he was strangled and choked with his own blood." A cardinal who hung Christians was himself hung in his cardinal's robes for all to see. When a man who murdered Christians was murdered in his own bed, "the just judgment of God showed itself." From Beard's perspective, these stories revealed "the wonderful judgments which the King of Kings has sent upon those that have in any place or country whatsoever resisted and strove against the Truth."[5]

---

2. See Walsham, *Providence in Early Modern England*, 115 and VanderMolen, "Providence as Mystery, Providence as Revelation," 27.

3. Quotes in this paragraph are taken from the preface of *The Theatre of God's Judgments.* Later Beard says "nothing happens by chance" (147) and sin "must needs draw after it a grievous and terrible punishment" (157).

4. Ibid., 42. On the next page, Beard qualifies his claim slightly, in stating that "generally few persecutors escaped without some evident and markable destruction" (43).

5. Ibid., 50, 58, 59, 66.

In Beard's view, those who fell away by backsliding or apostasy (renouncing the faith) could expect similar judgments from God. One man who verbally recanted his faith in Christ was "struck dumb and so was justly punished in that very member wherewith he had offended." After repudiating her faith with no remorse, a woman reportedly "chopped in pieces with her dainty teeth her rebellious tongue." Because a man named Lucian denied his earlier profession of Christianity "like a foul mouthed dog," fittingly "he was himself, in God's vengeance, torn in pieces and devoured by dogs."[6]

Biblical examples from the book of Acts are just the start of a longer pattern Beard saw for false teachers in the years ahead. When a bishop spoke "blasphemous words against the holy Trinity," in the year 510, "a threefold thunderbolt came from above and struck him dead in the same place," according to Beard's report. Mohammed, founder of Islam, was said to be judged for his heresies when "the Lord cut him off by the falling sickness." In Beard's narrative, the Anabaptists were also judged as "God scourged and plagued many of them" for "their monstrous and damnable heresies." According to Beard, God's judgments against various popes over the years included having their eyes pulled out, dying in prisons, dying of hunger, as well as being smothered to death, killed with the sword, stoned, poisoned, and stifled by the devil.[7]

While most of Beard's book focuses on the judgment of individuals, he also described God's judgments against groups of people. He said that at times God judges "one by one" but "other times altogether in a heap." According to Beard, in the middle of the third century, "the just hand of God" struck the Roman Empire with ten years of "plague and pestilence." And, while "the greatness of the plague touched also the Christians somewhat, yet it scourged the heathen idolaters much more." Over a millennium later, God judged the Eastern Empire for its idolatrous icons, according to Beard. The bloody massacre of Constantinople was, in his view, "the execution of God's most just wrath for idolatry." England had been under God's judgment for despising preacher John Wyckliffe's call to repentance; so the country experienced domestic turmoil, foreign war, civil discord, and economic decline—all of which Beard described as "extreme plagues of God's just vengeance!" Once a nation passed the tipping

6. Ibid., 71, 88.

7. Ibid., 100, 105, 137.

point of sin, Beard argued, God received glory by pouring out judgment on them.[8]

Such group judgments, however, paled in comparison to the bizarre punishments suffered by individual sinners. Beard told how a cruel tormentor of Christians "was shortly after so plagued of God that all the hair of his head and nails of his fingers and toes went off." Sabinianus, who taught a Trinitarian heresy, had his head suddenly fall from his shoulders without any human cause. When a twelve-year-old girl referred to God as "an old doting fool," Beard described how "the Lord in vengeance met with her" so that "suddenly she was struck dead, all the one side of her being black." When a man broke the Sabbath by habitually hunting on the Lord's day, "the Lord punished with this judgment: he caused his wife to bring forth a child with a head like a dog, that seeing he preferred his dogs before the service of God, he might have one of his own getting to make much of."[9] And these are just a small sampling from the first half of Beard's book, focused on the first four commandments. The second half of his book contains hundreds more spectacular stories of God judging people who broke the last six commandments.[10]

Most of us today are inclined to dismiss such stories as mere folklore. Like one Puritan scholar, we are skeptical of the "improbable correspondence between the mode of punishment and the nature of the crime."[11] In anticipation of such skepticism, Beard told his readers "that nothing is impossible to God" and "there is not one example here mentioned that

---

8. Ibid., 537, 31–32, 156–57, 202, preface.

9. Ibid., 65, 101, 184, 210.

10. Ibid., 214–592. Notable within the second collection are consecutive stories that warn against coveting. In the first story, when a farmer hoards his corn, "the Lord punished him with a strange and unusual judgment, for the corn which he so much cherished assumed life and became feathered fowls, flying out of his barns" which were left empty (478). In the second story, a governor refuses to sell his corn, though none could be purchased elsewhere—claiming he hardly had enough for his own hogs. But this "hoggish disposition the Lord requited in its own kind, for his wife at the next litter brought forth seven pigs at one birth to increase the number of his hogs" which he loved more than people (478–79). In Beard's stories, sinful disobedience may result in a human giving birth to a litter of seven little piglets!

11. Walsham, *Providence in Early Modern England*, 77. Walsham (70) argues that Beard's book "turns out to be a piece of wholesale plagiarism," and she documents many of the sources from which he drew his stories, notably Chassanion's 1581 compendium of judgment stories, *Des grands et redoutables jugements et punitions de Dieu advenus au monde principalement*, noted on the title page of Beard's 1597 edition.

does not have a credible or probable author for the voucher of it."[12] But beyond the issue of whether or not we can verify Beard's stories, it is important for the theme of our book that we analyze Beard's view of God's judgment in history.

DISCERNING GOD'S JUDGMENT IN CURRENT EVENTS

Within Beard's outlook, God's judgment continues in the present just as it did in "Bible times." He asked rhetorically, "if God spared not great cities, empires, monarchies, and kings in their obstinate misdeeds, shall we think he will spare little cities, hamlets, and villages, and men of bare estate, when by their sins they provoke him to anger?" The answer, to him, was obvious: "It cannot be, for God is always of one and the same nature, always like unto himself, *a God executing justice and judgment upon the earth*."[13] Since God has not changed, Beard reasoned, God's judgments on the earth must not have changed. Scripture shows us God's judgments in ancient times, and post-biblical history shows us God's judgments in all the centuries since then, including current events.

Beard and many Puritans believed that God directs the very details of the universe and "this a man may perceive." That is, humans can discern God's hand of providence in history. Especially when prominent people in this world who are proud and arrogant suffer a downturn, "in this we must acknowledge a special hand of God." It is worldly or "carnal" thinking to assign to blind chance what is really caused by God's power and providence. For example, when an official has a godly woman martyred and then a bull gores the official to death, Beard said we should "confess a plain miracle of God's almighty power and a work of his own finger." From his Puritan perspective, miracles are not shrouded in dark mystery, but instead are "plain," set out clearly for all to see.[14]

Beard believed that whenever a country or a person committed the sin of idolatry, the end result was ruin. In a sentence echoing the title and main idea of his book, Beard said that in history "God has propounded and laid open in this corrupt age a theater of his judgments, that every man might be warned thereby." The world is God's theater and on the

---

12. Beard, *Theatre of God's Judgments*, 213.

13. Ibid., 536, citing a verse from Jeremiah 23:5 (see also 33:15).

14. Ibid., preface, 8, 61. The last case is said to be "a plain demonstration of God's mighty power and judgment against a wretched persecutor of one of his poor flock" (61).

grand stage of history God performs judgments for all to observe. Beard said if we studied history rightly, God's judgments would leap off the pages and bring us wisdom.[15]

That raises the million-dollar question. Was Beard right? If we study history rightly, will God's judgments really be self-evident to us? Can we say, with strong confidence as Beard did, that "God was judging this person for that sin," or "God was judging this nation for that sin"? Can we truly perceive God's judgments in history?

Before evaluating Beard's outlook, we should note that he was representative of a broadly shared viewpoint. Dr. Thomas Beard was not a crackpot storyteller, but was a respected graduate from prestigious Cambridge University who served as a schoolmaster as well as an ordained minister. His book was widely read by Puritans in both England and New England, and it was followed by similar seventeenth-century works by other Puritans.[16] Beard's book is a great test case since it "holds pride of place in this revered literary tradition," was "cited in the margins of countless devotional works," and was "evidently a well-thumbed clerical reference book" used for sermon illustrations.[17]

On the popular level, many people of the day believed that God "regularly stepped in to discipline sinners and bestow blessings upon the righteous," and God's "finger could be discerned behind every inexplicable occurrence."[18] As one expert on Puritan thought said, there was "an enduring fascination with the wonder" so that reading God's judgments from providential signs was "the stuff of everyday experience."[19] As we evaluate

---

15. Ibid., 159, 188, preface.

16. See, for example, Samuel Clarke, *A Mirrour or Looking-Glasse both for Saints, and Sinners, Held forth in Some Thousands of Examples: Wherein is presented as Gods Wonderful Mercies to the one, so his severe Judgments against the other* (1646); Increase Mather, *An Essay for the Recording of Illustrious Providences* (1684), and William Turner, *A Compleat History of the Most Remarkable Providences, Both of Judgment and Mercy, Which Have Hapned in this Present Age* (1697).

17. Walsham, *Providence in Early Modern England*, 66.

18. Ibid., 2. Walsham concurs with Patrick Collinson that such beliefs were not unique to the Puritans, so that "the difference between their beliefs about divine activity and those of their neighbours and peers was essentially one of temperature rather than substance" (2).

19. Hall, *Worlds of Wonder, Days of Judgment*, 89. Walsham says, "nowhere is the Puritan propensity for detecting the finger of God in the most mundane events more vividly exhibited than in their journals and diaries, letters, autobiographies, and private memorabilia" (*Providence in Early Modern England*, 20).

Beard's outlook, then, we are assessing a viewpoint that was held by many. Also, because many American Christians are spiritual descendants of the Puritans, we are assessing a view that persists in many quarters today. As we will see at the end of the chapter, some twenty-first-century leaders closely echo Puritan perspectives on judgment.

POSITIVE ELEMENTS IN BEARD'S PURITAN PERSPECTIVE ON GOD'S JUDGMENTS

When we compare Beard's outlook with that of most people today (see chapter three), we see that Beard had a strong appreciation for the biblical image of God as judge. *Beard was well-versed in Scripture and his book accurately recounts dozens of instances in which the Bible says that God judged people for their sins.* Rather than downplaying what Scripture says about God as judge, as many do today, Beard unapologetically cast a spotlight on it. Though many examples could be cited, a few follow.

When Nadab and Abihu offered unauthorized fire, contrary to the Lord's command, fire came out from the presence of the Lord and consumed them to death. Because an Israelite blasphemed the name of the Lord, the Lord commanded that the community stone him to death. Likewise when a man broke the Sabbath, the Lord told Moses the man must die by stoning. When Uzzah irreverently took hold of the ark of God, the Lord's anger burned against him and struck him dead. Because King Jeroboam opposed a man of God, God made the king's hand shrivel up. When Elisha's servant wrongly took money and clothes from someone they helped, he was struck with leprosy. Because Nebuchadnezzar proudly boasted of all he had accomplished for his own glory, God drove him insane until he humbled himself before God. When King Herod allowed people to exalt him as a god and did not give proper praise to the true God, an angel of the Lord struck him down so that he was eaten by worms and died.[20]

Beard also drew readers' attention to what the Bible says about God's judgment of collective sin. When a group of Israelites rebelled against Moses and Aaron, the ground around the leaders and their families split apart so that they went down alive into the grave, and then fire came out

---

20. Beard, *Theatre of God's Judgments*, 161 (Leviticus 10); 179 (Leviticus 24); 208 (Numbers 15); 162–63 (2 Samuel 6); 81 (1 Kings 13); 108 (2 Kings 5); 128–30 (Daniel 4); 130 (Acts 12).

from the Lord and consumed 250 other men who supported these rebels. When the Israelites engaged in sexual immorality and worshipped foreign gods, the Lord's anger burned against them, and 24,000 people were killed in a plague. In a single day 120,000 soldiers in Judah were killed because they had forsaken the Lord. God judged both Israel and Judah for their idolatry by sending them into exile away from the Promised Land. In this way, Beard provided his readers with a sobering reminder that God had judged people's sins in the past and would continue to do so in the future. In Beard's words, because "God is always of one and the same nature, always like unto himself," God remains a God of justice who necessarily judges sin.[21]

Lastly, Beard had a strong appreciation for God's providence and vehemently denied that events occurred by mere chance. Since, as Jesus said, "not even a sparrow will fall to the ground apart from the will of your Father," Beard was right to take a countercultural stance against widespread notions of fortune or fate.[22] At a time when many people were fascinated with astrology, we can commend Beard for asserting that it is not "the stars" but God who directs the universe. The Bible teaches that God is providentially at work in the world; so we should not ascribe happenings to fate, luck, chance, or fortune—even if we do not immediately understand how God is at work in a particular event. In contrast to earlier medieval superstition and later Enlightenment skepticism, Beard and other Puritans were right to affirm that God sovereignly rules the world and human history. They properly promoted the biblical view that God is guiding and directing the creation, world history, and the personal circumstances of individuals. These positive elements, however, are countered by numerous problems in Beard's view.

NEGATIVE ELEMENTS IN BEARD'S PURITAN PERSPECTIVE ON GOD'S JUDGMENTS

First, though in theory Beard's book demonstrates how God blesses virtue and punishes vice,[23] in practice it mentions God's providential blessings only

21. Ibid., 161–62 (Numbers 16); 153 (Numbers 25); 84 (2 Chronicles 28); 154–55 (2 Kings 17, 24–25); final quote on 536.

22. Ibid., preface, 61, 147, 157. Jesus' statement is from Matthew 10:29. All biblical quotations in this book are taken from the New International Version, unless otherwise noted.

23. Ibid., preface.

in passing. Nearly all the space and attention are devoted to God's judgments. For Beard, "the key words were 'sin' and 'judgment,'" and his study of God's providence, for the most part, "revealed an angry God."[24] This comes out in the opening dedication, in which Beard stated that just as public hangings deterred others from crime, he hoped his book would "terrify us from these sins and bring us to repentance. God's quiver is full of venomed arrows, and his bow always bent, and when he shoots there is no way to escape."[25]

Anyone who reads the daily paper or watches the local news on TV realizes there is a bent toward the negative. Scandals, murders, violent crimes, and wars dominate the reporting, and little time is given to good news, since "bad news sells." Beard was not unique in this practice, as "sudden death, the gaping jaws of hell, a Christ who comes in judgment, the torments of despair—these themes were milked by printers and hack writers because of consumer demand."[26] On the other hand, Beard must be faulted for failing to keep God's judgment and God's love together in a wholistic way. His singular focus on divine wrath and vengeance fails to do justice to the fullness of who God is.

As we will see in later chapters, distorted theology is often associated with a distorted way of life. Puritans showed less charity overall than other groups in judging their neighbors' hearts before admitting them to church membership.[27] Some Puritans were also uncharitable when judging whether their neighbors were in league with the devil. Though it would be wrong to blame the Salem witch trials on Beard or other compilers of judgment stories, it is worth pondering whether their extraordinary focus on God as judge may have contributed in some way to Puritan judgmentalism toward others.

Second, while Beard conceded, in a passing note, that at times God "defers the punishment of the wicked" to the afterlife,[28] *the examples he piled up sent the cumulative message to readers that their sin would find them out and they might very well suffer a horrible judgment from God in this life.* The impression left by the bulk of Beard's six-hundred-page book is

24. Hall, *Worlds of Wonder, Days of Judgment,* 91 and 78.

25. Beard, *Theatre of God's Judgments,* dedication.

26. Hall, *Worlds of Wonder, Days of Judgment,* 134.

27. The shifting standards for church membership are documented in Tipson, "Invisible Saints," 460–71.

28. Beard, *Theatre of God's Judgments,* 537.

that there is nearly a one-to-one correspondence between human sin and earthly misfortune. In the words of one expert, Beard's book promotes a "crude providentialism in which suffering and misfortune are simplistically equated with immorality and sin."[29] When such a perspective is adopted, it can lead clergy to provide insensitive pastoral care by assuming that people's suffering is due to their personal sin.

As an example of insensitive pastoral care, consider that when two undergraduate students at Harvard were skating on a Sunday and broke through the ice, drowning to death, Puritan leader Increase Mather "was quick to note the moral: God punished Sabbath-breakers."[30] This incident became an opportunity to warn other students: "if you slight and make light of this hand of the Lord, or do not make a due improvement of it, you may fear, that God has not done with you, but that he has more arrows to shoot amongst you, that shall suddenly strike some of you ere long."[31] In this approach, when students die, one does not comfort the grieving classmates but instead warns them that they may suffer similar judgments of God. And Increase Mather was no renegade in his approach; most Puritan clergy saw instances of human calamity as ripe opportunities to preach God's judgment. Such an interpretive framework appears to "blame the victim" in a way that heaps more anguish on already tormented persons in need of comfort and support. This theology of judgment flies in the face of what we learn from Job—that catastrophe and suffering in a person's life are not sure indicators of God's disapproval. In Job's case, his suffering was not God's judgment of his sin but a test of his faith.

A third related problem is that throughout his book Beard moved seamlessly from Scriptural narratives into post-biblical history without differentiating between the two. The key difference, of course, is that in Scripture the divine interpretation typically accompanies the event. A prophet foretold what God was going to do and then God did it. Because the exiles of Israel and Judah were preceded by decades of divine forewarning, there could be no doubt that God was judging their sin. Or, alternatively in Scripture, God did something and then explained it afterward. For instance, God caused the Israelites to be defeated by an inferior army and when the lead-

---

29. Walsham, *Providence in Early Modern England*, 95.

30. Hall, *Worlds of Wonder, Days of Judgment*, 104.

31. Increase Mather, *A Discourse Concerning the Uncertainty of the Times of Men*, 347–48. While Mather refers to "the Rebuke of Heaven" (347) in this case, he does not assume that the skaters were eternally lost.

ers inquired about it, God clarified that the defeat was due to sin among the people.[32] No questions here. But there are plenty of questions about post-biblical events because God has not provided Scriptural interpretations of such events over the last nineteen centuries.[33]

Even in the day of Beard and the Puritans, interpreting current events proved to be a two-edged sword. Their reading of history could be flipped on its head and used against them. While Edward Johnson could marshal evidence of God's providential blessings upon New England, opponent Robert Child could point to God's providential curses (in numerous afflictions and premature deaths) that "signaled God's disfavor toward an 'evil' Massachusetts government." Increase Mather saw King Philip's War as a warning against people's declining spiritual fervor, but some Quakers viewed the same war as God's punishment against the Puritans who persecuted them. No matter what the happening of the day, "always there were clergy quick to read the meaning of these events, yet always someone proposed an alternative interpretation."[34]

Put simply, Beard and others were wrong to be as sure about God's judgments in recent events (when God did not provide a definite interpretation of what happened) as they were about God's judgments in biblical events (when God did provide a definite interpretation). How God works in history is not as plain as Beard claimed. Instead of presuming to know what has not been revealed to us, we should remember that "'my thoughts are not your thoughts, neither are your ways my ways,' declares the Lord."[35]

Fourth and most seriously, Beard and other Puritans appeared to interpret the events of post-biblical history in a self-serving way. It always seemed to be Beard's opponents who suffered God's judgments, but never Beard's allies or Beard himself. He devoted a section of his book to God's judgments on Jews who persecuted Christians, but never broached the subject of Christians who persecuted Jews. In nearly every section of

32. As an example, see Joshua 7—where the Israelites' defeat and loss of life at Ai was due to Achan's sin.

33. While affirming the biblical gift of prophecy described in 1 Corinthians and elsewhere, I do not believe we have divine interpretations of current events today comparable to the past events recorded in Scripture.

34. See Edward Johnson, *Wonder-Working Providence of Sions Saviour* (1654) and Hall, *Worlds of Wonder, Days of Judgment*, 103–04.

35. Isaiah 55:8.

Beard's book, Catholics, especially Catholic clergy, suffered God's judgment for mistreating Protestants, but never vice-versa. Anabaptists were scourged and plagued by God, but no mention is made of God judging those who persecuted the Anabaptists.[36]

Because so many people believed in God's providence, it was tempting to wield this doctrine as a weapon to promote one's own cause at the expense of one's opponents. All too often Puritans yielded to this temptation, as demonstrated by Increase Mather. His *Essay for the Recording of Illustrious Providences* (1684) followed in the tradition of Beard's *Theatre of God's Judgments* (1597).[37] Mather realized there was not a simple one-to-one correlation between human sin and earthly misfortune, since "the Lord's faithful servants have sometimes been the subjects of very dismal dispensations." Nonetheless, Mather believed that "a judgment may be so circumstanced as that the displeasure of heaven is plainly written upon it, in legible characters."[38] For Mather, as for Beard, God's providence was often "plainly written" in the circumstances of an event. God's judgments were essentially self-interpreting, clear for all to see.

Mather, like Beard, saw God's judgment in the lives of his opponents. He said that all wise people can "observe the blasting rebukes of providence upon the late singing and dancing Quakers." Mather thought that publishing God's judgments against the Quakers would show "all mankind that Quakers are under the strong delusions of Satan." Mather also discerned God's hand of judgment upon Native Americans who fought "the people of God in New England."[39] Just like Beard, Mather found it easy to spot God's judgment upon those with whom he disagreed. The danger here is that we simply use God's providence to reinforce the idea that we were right all along and now God has confirmed that we were right by judging our opponents' practices. And this temptation to declare "thus judgeth the Lord" is not restricted to the sixteenth and seventeenth centuries. It was not a problem just for the Puritans. Declarations of "thus

36. Beard, *Theatre of God's Judgments*, 43–49, 100.

37. Increase Mather, *An Essay for the Recording of Illustrious Providences* (Boston: Samuel Green, 1684), reprinted in the Garland Library of Narratives of North American Indian Captivities, volume 2 (New York: Garland Publishing, 1977), 340. By way of comparison, Mather focuses more on how God's providence is found in the natural, created order and recounts more instances of "positive providence" than does Beard.

38. Ibid., 338–39.

39. Ibid., 341, 345, 359.

judgeth the Lord" continue in the twenty-first century, as religious leaders still proclaim God's judgments in current events today.

ROBERTSON AND FALWELL ON GOD'S JUDGMENT IN THE TERRORIST ATTACKS OF 9/11

A dramatic example of the phenomenon of "thus judgeth the Lord" in our day is seen in the declarations put forth by prominent religious leaders Pat Robertson and Jerry Falwell after the attacks of September 11, 2001. Less than forty-eight hours after the attacks, Robertson made the following statement on his nationally televised show, *The 700 Club*:

> [W]e have allowed rampant pornography on the internet. We have allowed rampant secularism and occult, etc. to be broadcast on television. We have permitted somewhere in the neighborhood of 35 to 40 million unborn babies to be slaughtered in our society. We have a court that has essentially stuck its finger in God's eye and said we're going to legislate you out of the schools. We're going to take your commandments from off the courthouse steps in various states. We're not going to let little children read the commandments of God. We're not going to let the Bible be read, no prayer in our schools. We have insulted God at the highest levels of our government. And then we say "why does this happen?" Well, why it's happening is that God Almighty is lifting his protection from us.[40]

Minutes later, Robertson welcomed well-known religious leader Jerry Falwell as a guest on the show. Falwell stated that "the ACLU's got to take a lot of blame for this," to which Robertson replied "well, yes." Then Falwell made the following statement:

> And, I know that I'll hear from them for this. But, throwing God out successfully with the help of the federal court system, throwing God out of the public square, out of the schools. The abortionists have got to bear some burden for this because God will not be mocked. And when we destroy 40 million little innocent babies, we make God mad. I really believe that the pagans, and the abortionists, and the feminists, and the gays and lesbians who are actively trying to make that an alternative lifestyle, the ACLU, People for the American Way, all of them who have tried to secularize America.

40. Transcript of Pat Robertson's Interview with Jerry Falwell Broadcast on the 700 Club, September 13, 2001 in Lincoln, *Holy Terrors*, 108.

I point the finger in their face and say: "You helped this happen."
(Robertson then replied, "Well, I totally concur.")[41]

Later that evening Falwell gave a partial apology in a phone interview with CNN, but even then he stood by his link between the attacks of 9/11 and all the organizations "which have attempted to secularize America, [and] have removed our nation from its relationship with Christ on which it was founded."[42] To the sins of secularization and abortion that made God mad, Falwell added a list of offending groups (not focusing on the terrorists themselves!) that were to be blamed for helping the attacks of 9/11 happen.

As with Beard and Mather centuries ago, Robertson and Falwell also saw God confirming what they had been preaching for decades by judging their opponents' sinful practices. They had little hesitancy in responding to a contemporary tragedy by declaring "thus judgeth the Lord." And this view of 9/11 as God's judgment on America's sins has not been limited to popular religious leaders, but extends to established scholars as well.

VIA ON GOD'S JUDGMENT IN THE TERRORIST ATTACKS OF 9/11

Dan Via, a widely published professor emeritus of New Testament at Duke University Divinity School, recently wrote a book in which he argued "that one can make a plausible, tentative—but dialectical—case that 9/11 can and should be understood as divine judgment upon America." He believed that while 9/11 was clearly "an injustice, an evil, inflicted upon the U.S." it was also "a judgment against us for our violations of justice." Via cited the Old Testament pattern that when communities violate God's standard of justice then God judges them. In the case of the United States, "our action—injustice—leads to consequence—9/11." Via asserted that "the damage to America is to be seen as *judgment*" in the same way the exiles of Israel and Judah were divine judgment, using the metaphor of "the transcendent and holy God represented as a wrecking crew."[43]

Via acknowledged that we humans cannot fully fathom God's mysterious ways, and we are often self-deceived in our judgments due to our

41. Lincoln, *Holy Terrors*, 110.

42. Apology transcript available at http://archives.cnn.com/2001/US/09/14/Falwell.apology.

43. Via, *Divine Justice, Divine Judgment*, 3, 4, 59, 78 (italics in the original).

own blinding self-interests. So, he said, "we should be tentative and hesitant in making that assertion" of "9/11 as an event of judgment." In the end, though, when responding to the question of whether 9/11 was God's judgment on America, Via answered in the affirmative.[44] His book asserts that 9/11 was a warning for America to change if further disaster is to be avoided.

The second half of Via's book details new directions the United States must take "in order to achieve justice and, hopefully, turn aside an unwanted ending." In domestic affairs, Via said, we must establish universal health care, reduce the disparity between rich and poor, institute a living wage, raise taxes on the wealthy, ensure the solvency of Social Security, and reduce consumption and debt. We must also address global warming, dismiss intelligent design as non-scientific, support abortion rights worldwide, provide proper sex education, increase our pursuit of social justice, restrain the expansion of presidential power, and protect civil liberties against internal surveillance. Via said the main culprits in these problems were the Bush administration and the Christian Right.[45]

In foreign affairs, Via argued, we must repent of American imperialism over the past century—seen supremely in the war with Iraq. According to Via's book, American imperialism drives excessive military spending, the approved torture of prisoners, and the pursuit of corporate profit at the expense of proper care for workers and the environment. Here the list of culprits includes neoconservatives, the Christian Right, the World Bank, the World Trade Organization, the International Monetary Fund, and the Bush administration—which denied the truth and wreaked horrific evil upon the world.[46]

Via claimed that if the United States continues not to heed the warning of 9/11 we can expect a decline marked by ecological collapse, economic breakdown, and/or a slide into political fascism led by a tyrannical president. On the other hand, his book offers hope that "none of these possible scenarios is inevitable, if we have the courage and will to act" since "God is the hidden power directing this process." According to Via, we should use a rigorously progressive income tax and other government interventions to redistribute wealth so that everyone has adequate

44. Ibid., 5, 25, 71, 74, 77, 80.
45. Ibid., 84, 87–99, 101–14.
46. Ibid., 115–48.

food, clothing, housing, education, health care, and income. He further argued that we should punish companies that damage the environment and reward those that protect it. Lastly, we should reverse American imperialism that tries to make the rest of the world embrace our ideals. By these means, said Via, we can reflect the justice God requires of us, and "if we reshape society justly, we may avert the eruption of inequality and division into anarchy and chaos."[47]

Though Via's analysis is much more detailed than those of Beard and Falwell, his reading of history, like theirs, often villanizes others. For Beard the villains were mainly Roman Catholics, for Falwell mainly liberal Democrats, and for Via mainly conservative Republicans. In each case, God's judgment supposedly was activated chiefly by the evils of others. Both the cause (others' sin) and the cure (following "my way") confirm what was already believed before the supposed judgment. While representing opposite ends of the political spectrum, Falwell and Via each claimed that 9/11 was God's judgment on their opponents' practices, thus proving that their views were right. Declaring "thus judgeth the Lord" clearly is risky business. But should we rule it out altogether?

KEILLOR ON DISCERNING GOD'S JUDGMENTS IN HISTORY AND CURRENT EVENTS

Historian Steven Keillor, in a recent book, argued that our discernment of God's judgment may be imperfect and it is a difficult task, but "we have enough insight to avoid the agnostic view that we must take judgment off the table as an unknowable concept."[48] With this in mind, Keillor suggested that the British burning of Washington D.C. in 1814 was probably God's judgment of a pretentious, secular elite (especially Jefferson) who disdained the Christian faith. According to Keillor's analysis, we can be nearly certain that the Civil War was God's judgment of American slavery—"a terrible cup that God made the nation drink."[49] His book also offers a cautious "interpretation of September 11 as possibly God's judg-

---

47. Ibid., 149–56, 157, 158–82, with the last quote on 181.

48. Keillor, *God's Judgments*, 17. See also summary statements on pages 11, 48, and 60.

49. Ibid., 103–18, 119–53, quote from page 151. Keillor's thorough analysis includes details on how God used Garrisonians (139–41), the Free-Soil and Know-Nothings Parties (146–47), John Brown (149–50) and others specifically to accomplish God's intended judgments during this period.

ment on us for our materialism, our cultural exports seducing others into immorality and our use of terroristic guerilla units against the Soviets."[50]

Keillor is right that "Scripture teaches that God directs the course of events so as to give meaning to history, however difficult it often is for us to discern that meaning." He is also right that in the Old Testament the Lord is often revealed "as a God who uses historical events to punish collective, national evil." Keillor correctly points out that we cannot reject a theology of judgment just because some have abused it in the past. He recognizes that "warning of judgment is fraught with a potential for self-serving motives" and he insists that God judges sins and sinners regardless of their political affiliation.[51] These are all valid points, but Keillor's view still faces at least two serious objections.

The first objection concerns Keillor's effort "to correlate known causes of the event with known categories of divine holiness and judgment."[52] This "correlation approach" runs into problems when nations' sins do not match up neatly with God's judgments in history. As one scholar noted, "the Mexican War was a more egregious violation of divine standards than Jefferson's embargo, and yet in it the United States was successful." Or "why did God's judgment not fall on the nation after the end of Reconstruction in 1876 when once again a sinful subjugation of African Americans took place and with the full compliance of the American government and most American churches?"[53] Perhaps Psalm 73 provides a better perspective in not always looking for the judgment of the wicked in *this life*, when they may be wealthy and healthy, but seeing that their *final destiny*—if not in this life, then in the life to come—is utter destruction.

The second objection is that Keillor's approach presumes to know the mind of God. On the one hand, Keillor said that Scripture "alone is authorized to give God's interpretation of events," and the New Testament does not specifically identify God's judgments against the nations. On the other hand, Keillor was adamant that when "an event occurs that looks much like a judgment," Christians "must not back down from our diagnosis of divine judgment." The problem is obvious—if Scripture alone gives God's interpretation of events and Scripture does not comment on

50. Ibid., 35–60, quote from page 59. See also 187, 199–200.

51. Ibid., 19, 71, 162, 182, 191–97; final quote from page 188.

52. Ibid., 72.

53. Noll, "Foreword," in ibid., 9.

the burning of Washington, the Civil War, 9/11, or other recent events, it seems presumptuous of us to declare "thus judgeth the Lord" in these events.[54] Though the events *may* have been God's judgments, the problem is our presumption that we know the mind of God. But if we should not presume to know the mind of God, does that mean we have nothing at all to say about God's involvement in human history? Scripture provides us with four basic guidelines.

SOME BIBLICAL PRINCIPLES TO GUIDE US

1. We can affirm that God is providentially at work in history and in our lives. God is directing world history, even when we are not conscious of *how* God is doing it. In the words of Daniel, the Lord "changes times and seasons; he sets up kings and deposes them."[55] God even guides the lives of individuals and uses people to accomplish divine purposes. As the Lord said to Jeremiah, "before I formed you in the womb I knew you, before you were born I set you apart; I appointed you as a prophet to the nations."[56] So, against a bare deism in which God just winds up the clock and passively watches the world tick, we can affirm that God is actively directing world history and our own lives.

2. One way that God is providentially at work in history and in our lives is by judging sin. It started when God judged the first humans for their disobedience in the garden, and continued throughout the Old Testament as God judged individuals and nations for their sins, culminating with the exiles of Israel and Judah. The New Testament further reinforces the view that "the wrath of God is being revealed from heaven against all the godlessness and wickedness of men who suppress the truth by their wickedness." Besides God's ongoing judgment, Jesus frequently spoke of a final judgment to come.[57] From Genesis to Revelation, the Lord is consistently portrayed as a God who judges sin.

---

54. Ibid., 72, 86, 199–200. Keillor acknowledged this objection in passing but said that answering it was beyond the scope of his book (61).

55. Daniel 2:21. See also Job 12:23; Isaiah 10:5–13; Daniel 4:32–35.

56. Jeremiah 1:5. See also Esther 4:14; Proverbs 19:21; Acts 2:22–24, 4:27–28; Galatians 1:15–16.

57. Romans 1:18. For a survey of Jesus' teaching on the judgment to come, see chapter six of this book.

However, as a theologian recently reminded us, "it is one thing to say that there may be elements of God's judgment at work in the natural order as a result of prolonged human wickedness. It is another thing altogether to say that the people whose lives are snuffed out or devastated by a natural disaster are the ones deserving that judgment directly."[58] God is a judging God, but recognizing God's judgment is another matter.

3. *We know that an event was God's judgment when Scripture says so, but when we venture our own guesses about God's judgments, we are often mistaken.* The Bible frequently tells us that an event, such as the flood in Noah's time, was God's judgment of human sin. But when an event occurs without a divine interpretation, we are prone to presume wrongly that God is judging, even when that may not be true. Job's friends mistakenly believed that because the wicked suffer and Job was suffering, Job must be wicked. They even suggested sins for him to confess (impious speech, pride, oppression, and greed) so God would withdraw the hand of judgment from him.[59] The problem, of course, is the very first verse of the book tells us that Job was a blameless, upright, God-fearing person who shunned evil. Job did not suffer because of God's judgment of his sin, but rather because of a contest in the heavenly court between God and Satan. Satan said that Job feared God only because he was rewarded for it, and with a little adversity, Job would curse God. By the end of the book, Satan was proven wrong since Job still believed in God even though he received no instant benefits for it. Job was not just in it for the perks. Job's friends were also proven wrong for their false assumptions about God and their mistaken conclusion that Job's sufferings must be God's judgment on him.

4. *Jesus teaches us that people who suffer are not necessarily experiencing God's judgment for their sin, and we should concern ourselves mainly with our own spiritual condition.* John 9 tells the story of Jesus' encounter with a man blind from birth. Jesus' disciples asked him, "Rabbi, who sinned, this man or his parents, that he was born blind?" In their theology, this man's blindness must have been the result of sins committed by his parents or perhaps even by the man himself while he was still a baby in the womb. Those were their only two options—either the man sinned *in utero* or his

---

58. Wright, *God I Don't Understand*, 48.

59. Job, especially chapters 4, 5, 8, 11, 15, 18, 20, 22, 34, and 36.

parents sinned, producing his blindness. Jesus rejected both options. The man's blindness was not due to his sin or his parents' sin. Rather, the man's blindness happened so that the works of God might be revealed in him. Jesus taught his followers not to assume that personal suffering is always an indicator that God is judging personal sin.

In a final incident, recorded in Luke 13, people spoke with Jesus about some Galileans whom Pilate had killed. Jesus responded, "Do you think that these Galileans were worse sinners than all the other Galileans because they suffered this way? I tell you, no! But unless you repent, you too will all perish." Without a divine interpretation, we cannot conclude that people who die horrible deaths are especially horrible sinners. Instead we should see that we are all sinners who must repent or perish eternally. Jesus continued the lesson by bringing up another tragedy, in which eighteen people died when a tower in Siloam fell on them. His response here was similar: "Do you think they were more guilty than all the others living in Jerusalem? I tell you, no! But unless you repent, you too will all perish." Again, do not infer that people who suffer tragedies are uniquely guilty. Speculating about God's judgments on others often leads to wrong conclusions. Instead, Jesus said, look to yourself and recognize the need to repent from your own sin.

CONCLUSION

Many Puritans followed Thomas Beard's teaching that we can discern God's judgment in the events of our times. When something bad happened, it seemed obvious to them that God was sending heavenly judgment for earthly sin. Positively, most Puritans did not downplay what Scripture says about God as judge, as many do today. Negatively, Beard focused one-sidedly on God's judgment, while neglecting his love. Beard and others were also wrong to be as sure about God's judgments in current events (that mainly struck their opponents) as they were about God's judgments in biblical events.

Robertson, Falwell, and Via all interpreted the terrorist attacks of 9/11 as God's judgment on America's sins, though their lists of sins and sinners fell at opposite ends of the political spectrum. Keillor improved on these models by suggesting that God is an equal-opportunity judge across political lines, but his approach still faces the problems that nations' sins do not appear to match up neatly with God's judgments in this life, and we cannot presume to know God's mind. Scripture teaches us that God is providentially at work in history and in our lives, in part by judging sin. Scripture further teaches us, however, that when we hazard our own guesses about God's judgments in the events of our times, we are often mistaken. Rather than speculating about how God is judging others, Jesus directs our attention to our own sin and our own need to repent.

Clearly the whole business of trying to identify the Lord's judgments is fraught with peril. This chapter showed how we can fall into the mistake of presuming to know precisely how God is meting out judgment on people in current events. The next chapter will explore the related problem of people being terrorized by God's judgment while failing to grasp his love. The gripping story of Martin Luther shows us the way forward.

Questions for Reflection and Discussion

1. Share an example of a time when you heard a Christian leader or friend say that a current tragedy was probably God's judgment for sin (*and include your reaction*).

2. Which of Beard's judgment stories stands out the most to you? *Why this one?*

3. When, if ever, have you thought God was judging you, another person, or a group?

4. At a gut level, where do you think Robertson and Falwell were *on-track or off-track*?

5. Which biblical principle at the end is most *personally meaningful to you*? Explain.

6. How *should* Christians respond to catastrophes such as 9/11 or Hurricane Katrina?

From Harsh Judge to Loving Father

Lessons from Luther and Scripture

STRUGGLES WITH PICTURING GOD
AS AN UNLOVING JUDGE

PHILIP YANCEY IS ONE of today's best-known Christian authors, with nearly fifteen million books sold. His story reflects the struggle that many people face as they try to overcome a distorted view of God as an unloving judge. Yancey says, "I grew up in a strict, fundamentalist church in the Deep South, and was raised to view God as an abusive parent—rigid, legalistic, angry, ready to bring the gavel down for one wrong misstep." Yancey speaks of how these harsh images of God from his childhood scarred him. After a period of walking away from his faith, however, Yancey realized "God had been misrepresented to me," and he began the process of "recovery from bad church encounters." Now, he says, "I am learning to trust that God wants the best life for me in this world, not some diminished, repressed life."[1]

Correcting distorted images of God takes time. Yancey recovered only gradually (or he might say, is still recovering) from the "hellfire and brimstone church" of his youth. A major catalyst for Yancey's recovery was his involvement, as an adult, with a different church whose pastor "recognized his own endless need for grace, preached it almost every Sunday, and offered it to everyone around him in starkly practical ways."[2] Yancey

---

1. All information and quotes in this paragraph are taken from www.philipyancey.com.

2. Yancey, *Church*, 33.

describes how he came to know God's grace and love over thirteen long years.

> As I sat under his ministry Sunday after Sunday I gradually absorbed grace, as if by osmosis. I came to believe, truly believe, that God loves me not because I deserve it but because he is a God of grace. God's love comes free of charge, with no strings attached. There is nothing I can do to make God love me more—or less.[3]

Yancey's story is echoed through the centuries by thousands of others who have wrestled with the sense that God judges them and could not possibly love them. The first half of this chapter recounts the famous case of young Martin Luther, who was haunted for years by images of a harsh, judgmental God whom he could never satisfy. The second half of the chapter examines the antidote to this distorted view of God by exploring what Scripture teaches about God's love for sinners, even slave-trading sinners such as John Newton—who experienced God's amazing grace and celebrated it in song.

EARLY INFLUENCES THAT MAY HAVE SHAPED LUTHER'S IMAGE OF GOD AS A HARSH JUDGE

As a teen and throughout his twenties, Martin Luther could not love the God who seemed constantly to stand in judgment over him. Luther knew he was a sinner and that, because God is holy, God would judge him for his sin. What was there in this heavenly judge that might attract Luther? How could he, a sinful mortal, ever satisfy a God whose standard was perfection? Was it possible for him to love a righteous God who judged his unrighteousness? These questions haunted Martin Luther year after year after year.

Why? What was the source of Luther's image of God? Luther's parents, Hans and Margaret, provided for him and loved him. But they also punished young Martin in ways that produced bad memories which remained vivid into Luther's adulthood. In his own words, "my father once whipped me so that I ran away from him; I was upset until he was able to overcome the distance." Similarly, Luther reportedly said, "my mother caned me for stealing a nut, until the blood came. Such strict discipline drove me to the monastery, although she meant it well." As a young boy

---

3. Ibid., 33.

at school, Luther further related that, "I was caned in a single morning fifteen times for nothing at all. I was required to decline and conjugate [verbs in a language class] and hadn't learned my lesson."[4]

Many of Luther's biographers speculate that such encounters with authority figures at home and school may have shaped his view of God as a judge who punished him for all his shortcomings. Others caution against overstepping the evidence and making too much of the ways that negative childhood influences may have shaped Luther's later struggles with God.[5] After all, Luther's early years also had plenty of joy, including a good relationship with an older church vicar—clearly a positive father figure.

Whatever we make of Luther's upbringing, we know that the era in which he lived probably influenced his view of God. Luther "inhabited a universe in which they thought a threatening God kept a suspicious eye on every human act."[6] On daily walks as a student in his late teens and early twenties, he would have regularly passed a sculpture that "depicts Christ as a judge with a sword clenched between his teeth and a piercing stare."[7] Both God the Father and God the Son were frequently portrayed as harsh judges.

So, at age 21, when Luther was caught in the middle of a terrifying thunderstorm, he thought God was sending heavenly judgment on him. Fearing for his life, Luther did not call to God or Jesus, but rather cried out for help from Saint Anne—the mother of Mary who was thought to be a "helper in dangers from thunderstorms and from sudden death."[8] In the terror of the moment, face to face with his own mortality, Luther promised that in exchange for his deliverance from the storm, he would become a monk. If only his life could be spared, Luther pledged to quit his

---

4. Luther, *D. Martin Luthers Werke, Tischreden* vol. 2, no. 1559, 134 and vol. 3, no. 3566 B, 416. See Bainton, *Here I Stand*, 17.

5. Lohse, *Martin Luther's Theology*, 28–29. Brecht concurs that "one cannot say that Luther's relationship to God was decisively influenced and defined by the relationship to his father, and that his religious conflict was really a conflict with his father. The father did not wear the visage of an angry, judging God" (*Martin Luther*, 8–9).

6. Marty, *Martin Luther*, 14.

7. Nichols, *Martin Luther*, 26.

8. Brecht, *Martin Luther*, 49.

current studies as a law student (against his father's deep ambitions for his son) and instead enter the monastery.[9]

In late medieval times, the vow to become a monk or nun was commonly viewed as a "second baptism" that washed away all the sins a person had committed since his or her first baptism. Once a monk or nun, repentance would continually restore a person to a state of forgiveness so he or she would be assured of a place in heaven. Luther himself would later say, "I took the vow for the sake of my salvation."[10] Luther knew his father would disapprove of this career change (Hans initially threatened to disown Martin), and his friends tried to dissuade him. But two weeks after the storm, Luther threw a farewell party for his friends, and the next morning he made good on his vow to join a monastery.

FAILED EFFORTS AT FINDING SPIRITUAL PEACE

Alongside roughly fifty other monks in Erfurt, Germany, Luther was "turning away from the world and turning ascetically toward God" which entailed "killing off one's own will, meager meals, coarse clothing, hard work during the day, keeping vigil during the night, chastising the flesh, self-mortification by begging, extensive fasting, and an uneventful monastic life in one place." It was widely believed that "through masses, canonical hours, and rosaries, one could atone for sin, appease God, and become holy."[11]

Luther engaged in seven daily scheduled prayer gatherings, including one in the middle of the night, seeking God's grace and mercy. When conflicts during the week prevented him from attending, Luther would make up the prayer times on the weekend, though he always worried whether his prayers had truly satisfied the angry God. Later in life Luther criticized these prayer times for being rote rituals, not spoken from the heart.[12]

In order to come into the presence of a holy God, Luther believed a person must be holy. So Luther pursued holiness through every means the church prescribed. He prayed to the saints, took pilgrimages to holy sites, and participated in the sacraments. During his early years as a monk

9. Luther, *D. Martin Luthers Werke, Tischreden*, vol. 4, no. 4707, 440; vol. 4, no. 4707, 330; and vol. 5, no. 5373, 99.

10. Ibid., vol. 4, no. 4414.

11. Oberman, *Luther*, 127. Brecht, *Martin Luther*, 63–4.

12. Luther, *D. Martin Luthers Werke, Tischreden*, vol. 3, no. 3651.

Luther believed that "I had angered God, whom I in turn had to appease by doing good works."[13] With the other monks, Luther fasted every Friday year round, as well as some Wednesdays and Saturdays during special periods.

On a regular basis, often daily, Luther confessed his sins to a priest—with some sessions lasting several hours. But this practice could not still Luther's soul. Minutes later, Luther would recall other sins he had not confessed, or fear he had suppressed the memory of some sin, or worry he had not been genuinely sorrowful for his sin. Luther's scrupulous conscience harassed him with the nagging condemnation that he was never thorough enough in dealing with his sin. Spiritual anxiety set in with a vengeance. Reflecting on these years, Luther later related that he "feared hell somewhat; death, more; failure to please God the judge who made drastic demands, most: 'I trembled.'"[14]

Luther's restless soul lived in perpetual fear of God's harsh judgment. So, while on church business during a month-long trip to Rome, Luther sought spiritual strength in the renowned "holy city." Beyond routine devotions at the Roman monastery and daily masses at a local church, "there remained sufficient hours to enable him to say the general confession, to celebrate mass at sacred shrines, to visit the catacombs and the basilicas, to venerate the bones, the shrines, and every holy relic."[15] In an attempt to deliver his deceased grandfather from purgatory Luther even scaled "Pilate's stairs" on his knees. He paused to kiss each step and to repeat the Lord's prayer, but afterward he wondered if any spiritual good had been accomplished. His attempt to compensate for sins through the accepted channels in Rome failed to bring Luther the peace he sought.

The problem was not a lack of effort, but Luther's distorted view of God. When looking back on his fifteen years in the monastery, Luther said: "I was a good monk, and kept my order so strictly that I could say that if ever a monk could get to heaven through monastic discipline, I should have entered in. All my companions in the monastery who knew me would bear me out in this. For if it had gone on much longer, I would

13. Luther, *D. Martin Luthers Werke, Abteilung Werke*, vol. 47, 590.

14. Marty, *Martin Luther*, 16.

15. Bainton, *Here I Stand*, 37.

have martyred myself to death, what with vigils, prayers, reading and other works."[16]

Luther's spiritual mentor, Johann von Staupitz, and the writings of Christian mystics suggested another possible path to peace—union with God by becoming engulfed in the love of God. But Luther did not see how unholy people could be united to a holy God. In his mind, the chasm was unbridgeable. As one Luther scholar put it:

> Who, then, can love a God angry, judging, and damning? Who can love a Christ sitting on a rainbow, consigning the damned souls to the flames of hell? The mere sight of a crucifix was to Luther like a stroke of lightning. He would flee, then, from the angry Son to the merciful Mother. He would appeal to the saints—twenty-one of them he had selected as his especial patrons, three for each day of the week. All to no avail, for of what use is any intercession if God remains angry?[17]

Luther lived in constant dread of God as the harsh judge he could never please, and "when the Savior was mentioned, Luther recoiled from the very name, because it was only a synonym for the judge."[18] In Luther's mind, God was not the answer but the problem! Luther himself said, "I was myself more than once driven to the very abyss of despair so that I wished I had never been created. Love God? I hated him!"[19]

THE REVOLUTION: GOD'S LOVE IN CHRIST PROVIDES WHAT GOD'S HOLY JUDGMENT REQUIRES

How could he love a God who constantly stood in judgment of his sin? Luther found his answer in Scripture. Luther claimed never to have read a Bible before age twenty, but after entering the monastery he devoured Scripture. With the support and insistence of his mentor, Staupitz, Luther earned his doctorate in theology and was appointed as a professor of biblical theology. Luther studied the Bible intently as he prepared lectures for his students at the University of Wittenberg on the Psalms and the book of Romans.

---

16. Luther, *D. Martin Luthers Werke, Abteilung Werke*, vol. 38, 143 and vol. 40.II, 574. Cited in Steinmetz, *Luther in Context*, 7.

17. Bainton, *Here I Stand*, 43–4.

18. Brecht, *Martin Luther*, 78.

19. Cited in Bainton, *Here I Stand*, 44.

On the one hand, much of what Luther read in Scripture "reinforced the pictures in his mind of a holy, zealous, wrathful, and punishing God."[20] Luther remained convinced that we must humbly accept the verdict that we are sinners who deserve God's judgment of condemnation. On the other hand, in the Psalms Luther also discovered prophecies of a Messiah who would suffer for us, taking others' sin upon himself. For Luther, above all, the Psalms pointed to Christ and the Christ he found was appealing.

Luther still believed Christ judges sin in the sense that light necessarily exposes darkness. But now Luther saw in the Psalms that Christ came to identify with sinners and suffer in their place. Through his study of the Psalms, "a definite change certainly took place in Luther's image of God. No longer did he find himself in continual confrontation with the judging God," since he saw that "Christ's wounds assure us of God's love."[21]

This new understanding of God was further reinforced by Luther's study of the book of Romans. When he encountered the phrase "the righteousness of God," originally Luther took it to mean the righteousness "with which God is righteous and punishes the unrighteous sinner." He admitted candidly that "I did not love, yes, I hated the righteous God who punishes sinners, and secretly, if not blasphemously, certainly murmuring greatly, I was angry with God."[22] However, after meditating day and night on the context of Romans 1:17, Luther came to a new understanding of "the righteousness of God," one that would reverberate through centuries to come. He explains what happened.

> There I began to understand that the righteousness of God is that by which the righteous lives by a gift of God, namely by faith. And this is the meaning: The righteousness of God is revealed by the gospel, namely, the passive righteousness with which the merciful God justifies us by faith. . . . Here I felt that I was altogether born again and had entered paradise itself through open gates. . . . Thus that place in Paul was for me truly the gate to paradise.[23]

The cross accomplished what Luther called the sweet and joyful exchange between Christ's righteousness and the sin of all who have faith

---

20. Marty, *Martin Luther*, 21.

21. Brecht, *Martin Luther*, 136 and Oberman, *Luther*, 182.

22. Luther, *D. Martin Luthers Werke, Abteilung Werke*, vol. 54, 185–6.

23. Ibid., vol. 54, 186. Similar reflections are found in *D. Martin Luthers Werke, Tischreden*, vol. 4, no. 4007, 73.

in him. Believers' sin was borne by Christ so that we bear it no more, and Christ's righteousness was credited to our account so God can truly declare us to be justified by faith in what Christ has done for us. Put simply, "through faith in Christ his righteousness becomes our righteousness, and everything which belongs to him becomes ours. This is the meaning of Rom 1:17."[24]

The righteousness that God requires could not be produced by sinners. Instead it must be received as God's gift to sinners through Christ. So a believer is simultaneously a sinner and righteous in God's sight through Christ's gracious redemption.[25] This was the gospel that could bring rest to Luther's troubled soul! God judges sin because God is holy, but God provides forgiveness of sin through Christ's death because God is loving.

Though scholars debate the exact date of Luther's "Reformation discovery," they agree that some time during his early thirties Luther moved from hating the God who judged him to loving the God who redeemed him. The Scriptural teaching that people are saved purely by God's grace through faith in Christ was exceptionally good news for Luther and for thousands of others who embraced this message. After suffering years of spiritual anguish, Luther ultimately came to the revolutionary insight that God's love in Christ provides the perfect righteousness that God's holy judgment requires.[26]

On October 31, 1517, Luther posted the famous ninety-five theses, which objected to several practices in the church of his day, including the sale of indulgences—which in its worst form, had degenerated into buying forgiveness of sins. In simple terms, according to the theology of the time, those who were sorry for their sins and had confessed them could pay money to church officials, who would issue a certificate declaring that satisfaction had been made for their sins and they (or their deceased loved ones) would not have to suffer in purgatory—an unpleasant way station en route to heaven.

---

24. Brecht, *Martin Luther,* 229. See also *D. Martin Luthers Werke, Abteilung Werke,* vol. 50, 198.

25. Luther, *D. Martin Luthers Werke, Abteilung Werke,* vol. 56, 272.

26. Oberman observes that Luther arrived at his world-shattering insight through "the simultaneous struggle of religious experience, practical life, and scholarly penetration" (*Luther,* 158). While Luther was profoundly changed, Steinmetz rightly notes that "even after the great shift in his theological outlook, Luther continued to suffer periods of severe spiritual anxiety" (*Luther in Context,* 1).

Luther railed against the slogan, "a penny in the box, a soul out of purgatory." If the pope could really deliver souls from purgatory, Luther said in the eighty-second of the ninety-five theses, he should empty the place immediately and free of charge! Indulgences had degenerated into corrupt fundraisers, even promising mercy to one's deceased relatives with the advertising pitch, "as soon as the coin in the coffer rings, the soul from purgatory springs." Luther feared that indulgences gave people false assurance that their sins were forgiven and blinded them to the true gospel of Christ. Thousands of people rallied behind Luther and a popular groundswell of support for his cause mushroomed.

Within a couple of months Luther's theses had been published in several leading cities, using newly developed technology in the printing press. They spread like wildfire and spurred a widespread social movement Luther had not foreseen. He said, "God led me into this business against my will and knowledge."[27] The backlash was strong and within a few years Luther endured "triple expulsion" as he was released from his vows of monastic obedience (by Staupitz), excommunicated from the Roman Catholic Church (by the pope), and banned as an outlaw in the Holy Roman Empire (by the emperor).

Over time Luther had been transformed from a fearful monk into a bold, but very imperfect, reformer.[28] In the end, Luther could love a holy God who judges our sin because that same God lovingly sent his Son to atone for our sin, bringing us the gracious gift of salvation, received by faith. For the sake of his spiritual health, Luther needed the whole truth—that God is a holy judge of sin *and* a loving father who provides the means of forgiveness to his children. Like Luther, we continue to need the whole truth today.

WE NEED THE TRUTH, THE WHOLE TRUTH, AND NOTHING BUT THE TRUTH—SO HELP US GOD

Half-truths can be hazardous to our health. In the physical sphere, consider the old adage, "feed a cold and starve a fever." The half-truth is we should feed a cold because proper nutrition can help our bodies recover from the viral infections that cause colds. But the second half of the adage

27. Luther, *D. Martin Luthers Werke, Tischreden*, vol. 1, no. 1206.

28. Luther's harsh rhetoric and his views of popes, Jews, and the Peasant's Revolt are widely documented.

is false. We should not starve a fever because "when your temperature goes up, so does your metabolism—which means your body requires calories more than ever to carry out basic functions like breathing and pumping blood. Not eating will only make it harder for your body to fight off the illness."[29]

In the spiritual sphere, we also need to move beyond half-truths to embrace the whole truth. In the New Testament, John's first letter declares, "if we claim to be without sin, we deceive ourselves and the truth is not in us." Admitting our sin is a huge step, but it gets us only halfway there spiritually. By itself, awareness of sin may lead to despair, as it did for young Luther. So, under the inspiration of the Holy Spirit, John was quick to add the rest of the truth in the very next verse: "if we confess our sins, God is faithful and just and will forgive us our sins and purify us from all unrighteousness."[30]

Young Martin Luther, Philip Yancey, and many others have experienced a vivid sense that we are sinners before a holy God. But the first half of the truth—that we are spiritually ill—is only a prelude. The second half of the truth is that God supplies the spiritual cure! We need the whole story, which tells us that we are sinners before a holy God *and* that God loves sinners so much that he has provided a way for us to be forgiven of our sins. We need to absorb into the very depths of our being that God saves sinners because God *is* love. The sweet truth of God's love is taught over and over in Scripture.

Of the 31,000 verses in the Bible, one of the best known is John 3:16, a verse which Luther called the gospel in miniature: "For God so loved the world that he gave his one and only Son, that whoever believes in him shall not perish but have eternal life." Because this is such a familiar verse, we risk being dulled to how profound it is. God's love is so extravagant that God gave his unique, only Son as a priceless gift to the world. Out of immense love, God sent his Son to come down from heaven and ultimately to be lifted up on the cross, where he would endure an excruciating death so that sinners could be forgiven. God's love is a sacrificial love—giving what was most precious to him so that anyone in the world who believes in his Son should not perish but have eternal life.

---

29. Snyderman, *Medical Myths That Can Kill You*, 49.
30. 1 John 1:8–9.

KNOWING THAT GOD IS LOVE

The New Testament letter of 1 John says, "God is love. This is how God showed his love among us: He sent his one and only Son into the world that we might live through him. This is love: not that we loved God, but that he loved us and sent his Son as an atoning sacrifice for our sins." As one theologian said, "the measure of love is how much it gives."[31] By this standard God's love is enormous, because God the Father gave what was most valuable to him—his only Son, who would die to save people from their sins.

In case we missed it the first time, a few verses later John says that we can "know and rely on the love God has for us. God is love." God's people know that because God *is* love, God expresses love in all that he does. In fact, we could say that God is *never not love*. God is and forever will be love, one hundred percent of the time. So, "even when we cannot see the why and the wherefore of God's dealings, we know that there is love in and behind them, and so we can rejoice always, even when, humanly speaking, things are going wrong."[32]

Think about people who have been thrown into prison even though they are totally innocent of wrongdoing—a situation the apostle Paul endured many times during his life. Even when, humanly speaking, things were going wrong, Paul never doubted God's love, and he wanted others to know the incredible dimensions of God's love. So, when Paul was in prison, an ambassador for Christ in chains, he prayed for the believers in and around the ancient city of Ephesus that "you, being rooted and established in love, may have power, together with all the saints, to grasp how wide and long and high and deep is the love of Christ, and to know this love that surpasses knowledge—that you may be filled to the measure of all the fullness of God."[33] That is a prayer worth pondering.

Stuck in prison with plenty of time to kneel in prayer before his heavenly Father, Paul did not feel sorry for himself, but retained an outward focus on others by asking that God might allow the believers in the vicinity of Ephesus to fathom the unfathomable love of Christ. By combining agricultural and architectural imagery, Paul saw love as "the soil in which

---

31. 1 John 4:8–10 and Packer, *Knowing God*, 125.

32. 1 John 4:16 and Packer, *Knowing God*, 117, 123.

33. Ephesians 3:17–19.

believers are to be rooted and grow" as well as "the foundation on which they are to be built."[34] Love is at the very center of Paul's prayer.

Specifically, Paul prayed that collectively ("together with all the saints") these believers might experience a better sense of the extent of Christ's love.[35] It is crucial to notice that "this is not a petition that they may love Christ more, however important this might be; rather, that they might understand Christ's love for them."[36] Way back in the first century, the Ephesians needed what Luther, Yancey, and many of us need today—a heart-penetrating grasp of God's mind-boggling and life-transforming love in Christ.

By using four measurements (width, length, height, and depth) to describe the love of Christ, Paul's point seems to be that it is infinite and cannot be measured. As one commentator said, Paul prays that the Ephesian Christians might "know the love that is beyond knowing."[37] We will never fully comprehend God's love for us but, like Paul, we can plead with God that we might know this love more and more.

Rather than being discouraged that we cannot fully grasp God's love, we can see it as an exciting adventure without end. John Bunyan, famous author of *Pilgrim's Progress*, encouraged Christians to "be much in the study and search after the greatness of this love." A contemporary Bible scholar agrees: "no matter how much we know of the love of Christ, how fully we enter into his love for us, there is always more to know and experience."[38] So, we need to pray this prayer as much today as ever.

Paul's prayer culminates with the request that the Ephesians "may be filled to the measure of all the fullness of God." Wow! That's praying big! Paul's prayer teaches us that God's people "may enter into the total fullness of God" as we "increasingly come to understand and be penetrated by the love of Christ." The bottom line for Christians is that "their nature and

---

34. Lincoln, *Ephesians*, 207.

35. Various scholars have suggested that Paul is praying for the readers to grasp the extent of God's power, God's wisdom, the universe, heaven, the mystery of salvation in Christ, or the cosmic magnitude of the cross. However, "the most popular view among commentators has been to understand the object of the four dimensions as the love of Christ, which is explicitly mentioned in the following clause, v. 19a" (O'Brien, *Letter to the Ephesians*, 263). Lincoln's thorough discussion concludes that "a reference to the love of Christ is probably to be preferred" (*Ephesians*, 213).

36. O'Brien, *Letter to the Ephesians*, 264.

37. Snodgrass, *Ephesians*, 182.

38. Bunyan, *All Loves* Excelling, 107, 112. O'Brien, *Letter to the Ephesians*, 264.

God's should coincide but this can only happen when God fills them with his love."[39] God's love is the key from start to finish. God's love nourishes believers, transforms them, and allows them to be filled with the fullness of God! And if we want the clearest possible picture of God's love, we just need to look at Jesus Christ.

JESUS CHRIST AS THE CRYSTAL CLEAR PICTURE OF GOD'S LOVE

Something about Jesus caused sinners to gather around to hear him. By contrast, "the Pharisees and the teachers of the law muttered, 'This man welcomes sinners and eats with them.'" Jesus responded to these religious leaders by telling a series of three related parables. In the first, a shepherd leaves ninety-nine other sheep to go after one that was lost. The story ends with rejoicing in heaven over one sinner who repents—which shows why Jesus was right to reach out in love to lost sinners. Likewise in the second parable a woman is naturally concerned about her one lost coin, and the story ends with heavenly joy over a repentant sinner—like the ones Jesus welcomed and ate with. *The point is that like the shepherd and the woman, Jesus lovingly sought out what is valuable and is lost.*[40]

The third parable is longer and allows us to see God's love for lost people in more detail. The Father's love for his lost (prodigal) son pictures God's love for lost sinners. Especially striking is the statement that while the lost son "was still a long way off, his father saw him and was filled with compassion for him; he ran to his son, threw his arms around him and kissed him." For a middle-eastern father to run and greet a wayward son would be considered improper (just as a Jewish rabbi eating with sinners was), which is precisely why Jesus chose this figure to illustrate God's radical love for lost people.

The father's warm hug, kisses, robe, ring, sandals, and feast picture God's full acceptance of repentant sinners. God's love for lost people is undeserved, extravagant, and shocking—as was Jesus' scandalous outreach to sinners. The religious leaders of Jesus' day did not get it. So Jesus' parable included a third figure, the older brother, who would not join the celebration. The negative example of the older brother teaches the

---

39. Schnackenburg, *Ephesians: A Commentary*, 144, 152. Best, *Ephesians*, 348.

40. Luke 15:1–10. Jesus describes his mission to lost sinners in similar terms in Luke 5:31–32 and 19:10.

Pharisees (and us!) not to stand in judgment of God's grace toward others, but instead to happily embrace repentant sinners just as God does.[41] All three stories invite us to join in joyous celebration with people who once were lost but now are found because a God of abundant, lavish love has taken the initiative to seek and to save sinners.

GOD'S SAVING LOVE IN CHRIST ILLUSTRATED— NEWTON'S STORY

John Newton was one such sinner, saved by God's amazing grace. His mother nurtured him in the Christian faith as much as she could during his early years, but she died of tuberculosis when Newton was just six years old. His father, a ship captain, was quickly remarried to a younger woman, and they sent Newton away to a boarding school for a couple of years. Once he reached his pre-teen years, Newton was allowed to accompany his father on voyages in the Mediterranean. By age seventeen, Newton had fallen in love with Mary Catlett, but he could not pursue the relationship because she was a mere thirteen-year-old and he was often out at sea. Newton himself reports that he idolized his new love in such a way that "it greatly weakened my sense of religion."[42]

Newton's "sense of religion" was weakened even further in the years ahead. During a day ashore, Newton was caught trying to desert his ship, which led to his public whipping and imprisonment. Newton's spirits were so low that he said, "I was tempted to throw myself into the sea, which would put a period to all my sorrows at once." One of Newton's biographers relates that he was kept alive mainly by the "resolve that he would not commit suicide before murdering the captain who had humiliated him. He was convinced that there was no life after death when he would be held accountable for dastardly deeds." Newton reported that he did not follow through on his plan because, "though I neither feared God, nor regarded men, I could not bear that she [Mary, his love] should think so meanly of me when I was dead."[43]

Things got worse before they got better. After Newton was put on another ship, he began to pursue slave trading and recounted that "from this time I was exceedingly vile" to such a degree that he was ashamed

41. Luke 15:11–32.
42. Newton, *Works of the Rev. John Newton*, 1:17.
43. Ibid., 1:23, 1:25. See Phipps, *Amazing Grace in John Newton*, 9.

to give the details. By his own report, during his early twenties Newton was a slave to wickedness, who delighted in sin. Then during one night in March 1748, Newton was awakened both physically and spiritually. A violent storm struck Newton's ship and threatened to sink it. Face to face with death, as he pumped water in despair and reviewed his miserable life, Newton said, "I thought if the Christian religion were true, I could not be forgiven." After several anxious days, the ship survived, but both Newton and his captain wondered if God had directed the storm at this disobedient sinner, as in the story of Jonah. And like Jonah, Newton felt he had been "snatched, by a miracle, from sinking into the ocean and into hell."[44]

Looking back, Newton reported that "I consider this as the beginning of my return to God, or rather of his return to me." He likened himself to the prodigal son who indulged in riotous living before bottoming out, coming to his senses, and experiencing unexpected love and acceptance when he returned home to his father.[45] Newton began to pray and read the Bible regularly, stopped swearing, and married his love, Mary Catlett.

His full repentance from sin, however, took much longer. For the next five years Newton continued slave trading between Africa and the West Indies, as a first officer and then as a commander of his own ship. Somehow he was able to engage in devotional activities in his captain's quarters and lead Sunday worship on the main deck, while hundreds of slaves suffered extreme, inhumane treatment and often died in the lower decks. Only later in life, perhaps as a result of his friendship with John Wesley and others, did Newton come to realize that "slave trade was inimitable to basic Christian ethics" and to work for its abolition. Serving alongside others, Newton was especially valuable to the abolitionist cause since "he knew the slave-trade business inside out" and could provide "invaluable firsthand knowledge of what was being opposed."[46]

Looking back on his own slave-trading days, Newton expressed wonder that "I did not at the time start with horror at my own employment as an agent in promoting it. Custom, example, and [economic] interest had blinded my eyes."[47] In the words of Newton's most famous hymn,

44. Newton, *Works of the Rev. John Newton*, 1:27, 1:41. Newton, *Twenty-five Letters of the Rev. John Newton*, 69.

45. Ibid., 1:46, 1:48.

46. Phipps, *Amazing Grace in John Newton*, 178, 183.

47. Newton, *Works of the Rev. John Newton*, 4:72.

"Amazing grace, how sweet the sound, that saved a wretch like me. I once was lost, but now am found, was blind, but now I see." While he said, "the greater part of my life has been a series of repeated backslidings," Newton also gave thanks to God that, "my whole life has been a signal display of Thy goodness and care."[48]

Newton had come to know the whole truth—that God judged his sin as wrong but lovingly forgave him because of Christ. God opened Newton's eyes to his disease of sin ("twas grace that taught my heart to fear") as well as to the cure in Christ ("and grace my fears relieved"). Newton then served for decades as a pastor, and at his request, had his monument inscribed: "John Newton, clerk, once an infidel and libertine, a servant of slaves in Africa, was, by the rich mercy of our Lord and Saviour Jesus Christ, preserved, restored, pardoned, and appointed to preach the faith he had long laboured to destroy."[49] Shortly before his death, Netwon reportedly said, "My memory is nearly gone, but I remember two things: That I am a great sinner and that Christ is a great Savior!" John Newton knew in the very depths of his soul the whole truth that God loves sinners.

JESUS DEMONSTRATES GOD'S LOVE IN ACTION

John's Gospel says that "God did not send his Son into the world to condemn the world, but to save the world through him."[50] John goes on to describe God's radical love in Christ. Think of chapter thirteen, which says of Jesus, "having loved his own who were in the world, he loved them to the end." Jesus loved people to the very last days of his life, and during his final earthly hours he showed them the full extent of his love. Even though Jesus knew that one of his disciples would betray him, a second would deny him, and the others would desert him, he still showed them nothing but love right to the end.

We are told that Jesus got up from the last supper and took off his outer clothing, which probably left him wearing only an inner tunic—something like a long undershirt. Then he wrapped a long towel or linen cloth around his waist, dressed as a slave for the work of a slave. In so do-

---

48. Newton, "Diary of John Newton," 2:314 and 2:327. Cited in Phipps, *Amazing Grace in John Newton*, 205 and 207.

49. Cited in Hindmarsh, *John Newton and the Evangelical Tradition*, 14.

50. John 3:17.

ing, Jesus assumed what was considered the demeaning role of the lowest servant. Amazingly, "there is no parallel in extant ancient literature for a person of superior status voluntarily washing the feet of someone of inferior status."[51] And even though he knew that Judas was soon to betray him and Peter was soon to disown him, Jesus lovingly washed their feet right along with the other disciples.

Beyond washing their feet, Jesus showed his supreme love for sinners by dying in their place—as the good shepherd who laid down his life for the sheep. Greater love has no one than this—that he lay down his life for his friends, even when those friends are undeserving sinners. Contextually we know that "in the ancient world outside Christianity, it was thought appropriate to love only those who were regarded as worthy of being loved. But God loves sinners who are unworthy of his love, and indeed subject to his wrath. He loved us and sent his Son to rescue us, not because we are lovable, but because he is love."[52] God loves sinners simply because God's very nature is love.

In fact, God loves people so much that when we receive God's love in Christ, by turning away from our sins (repentance) and trusting what Christ has done for us (faith), God actually adopts us into his family of love. John's Gospel teaches that from all eternity, love has flowed freely between God the Father and God the Son. Even more mind-boggling, God wants to include people in this unending fellowship of love! Because God's nature is love, he desires to incorporate others in his eternal kingdom of love.[53]

Jesus concluded his longest recorded prayer in Scripture by expressing his desire that all who believe in him be completely united in love. Jesus wanted (and still wants!) the love that the Father has for him to be in his followers. The world can then come to know the God of love through our verbal proclamation of the gospel and through the visible witness of

---

51. Lincoln, *Gospel according to Saint John*, 367.

52. John 10:11–15, 15:13. Stott, *Letters of John*, 165–166.

53. John 1:12, 3:35, 5:20, 10:38, 14:10, 14:31, 15:9. The Spirit's participation in the eternal divine love must be inferred. Because the Spirit is a distinct Person (Acts 13:2, 1 Corinthians 12:1–11, Ephesians 4:30) who is fully divine (Matthew 28:19, Acts 5:3–4, 1 Peter 1:2), it stands to reason that the Spirit also participates in eternal love with the Father and the Son, though no single biblical text, by itself, establishes this claim.

our unity with each other. When God's children are united in love, we are "an advertisement, inviting people to join in this union with God."[54]

Of course, God's people have often failed miserably at this task of being united in love. As the saying goes, "to live above with saints we love, that will be glory. To live below with saints we know, well that's another story." All too frequently God's children have engaged in unhealthy sibling rivalry and even worse toward those outside the family of God. One day, however, God's people will be perfected in heaven. And with that prospect in mind, John explodes with excitement: "how great is the love the Father has lavished on us, that we should be called children of God. And that is what we are!"[55]

OUR RESPONSE TO GOD'S LOVE

When we have received God's love and have been adopted into God's family of love, we are moved to respond in love. God takes the initiative in loving us, and we answer by gratefully loving God and other people. John's first letter says when we have embraced Jesus as God's Son and our Savior, we rely on the love God has for us and face the day of judgment with confidence (4:14–17). While we continue to revere God, we no longer cringe in fear of God, but instead we respond with love because God first loved us (4:18–19). As opposed to the "servile fear" of a slave who cowers before a harsh master, Christians should have a "filial fear" which is "that indefinable mixture of reverence, fear, pleasure, joy and awe which fills our hearts when we realize who God is and what He has done for us."[56] As God's grace transforms our hearts, we are enabled to receive and give love, as God designed us to. First we receive God's love for us, and then we live in the overflow of God's love—by loving God and other people.

The more we meditate on God's incalculable love for us, the more our hearts burn with a responsive love for God. Affection for God wells up in our hearts. Praise to God pours forth from our lips. Obedience to God characterizes our lives. As we take in and rest in God's love, we are moved from the terror of a fearful slave (young Luther) to the willing obedience of a child who wants to please his or her heavenly Father. As

---

54. John 17:20–26. Whitacre, *John*, 420.

55. 1 John 3:1. The next verse refers to the future perfection of God's people at Christ's return.

56. Ferguson, *Grow in Grace*, 36.

Luther said, once saving faith and love for God are present, we can freely and joyfully do good works for God's glory. We can even measure the temperature of our responsive love for God by the thermometer of our obedience to God.[57]

A second way we respond to God's love is by loving other people. In fact, loving others within God's family is a sign that we have passed from death to life. Just as Jesus laid down his life for us, so we ought to lay down our lives for other members of our spiritual family. This means not merely loving with words, but loving with concrete actions. Within the theology of John's first letter, God's central command to humans can be compressed into two points: "to believe in the name of his Son, Jesus Christ, and to love one another as he commanded us." Of course, this is easier said than done. There are hard questions to be faced. A contemporary pastor posed these hard questions in no-nonsense terms: "How can we be kind to the vow breakers? To those who are unkind to us? How can we be patient with people who have the warmth of a vulture and the tenderness of a porcupine? How can we forgive the moneygrubbers and backstabbers we meet, love, and [sometimes even] marry? How can we love as God loves?"[58]

The Bible answers these questions by telling us that on our own we *cannot* love difficult people, especially our enemies, as God does. Rather, God must pour his love into our hearts so that his love can overflow from us to others. Love is something the Holy Spirit produces in our lives.[59]

It is absolutely amazing that while he was being crucified that Jesus kept his focus outward and showed the composure and love to pray for his executioners, "Father, forgive them, for they do not know what they are doing."[60] I want to love people with that sort of radical love. But I know the only way I will ever be able to love like that is for God to love through me. I cannot do it on my own. God's love is the answer.

---

57. See Luther's 1520 sermon *On Good Works* and his 1520 treatise *Freedom of a Christian*. John 14:15, 14:21, 14:23, 14:31.

58. 1 John 3:10–11, 3:14, 3:16–18, 3:23. Lucado, *A Love Worth Living*, 9.

59. Romans 5:5; Galatians 5:22.

60. Luke 23:34. See the similar account of Stephen in Acts 7:59–60.

CONCLUSION

Martin Luther shows us just how terrifying it can be to believe in a God of judgment who is not also a God of love. It is impossible for us to find spiritual peace when we are living in constant dread of God as the harsh judge whom we can never please. Thankfully, Luther also teaches us the incredible wonder of coming to know God's love for us. When we realize that God's love in Christ provides what God's holy judgment requires, it is truly as though the gates of paradise have been opened to us. We need the whole truth of Scripture: that we are spiritually ill and deserving of judgment for our sin because God is holy, but that God provides the spiritual cure and offers us forgiveness of sin because God is love.

Though we will never fully comprehend God's love for us, following Paul's example we can plead with God that we might know this love more and more—seeing it as an exciting adventure without end. Jesus gives us a crystal clear picture of God's love—in the way he related to sinners, served his disciples, and laid down his life for those who deserved to be separated from God forever. When we receive the eternal life that Christ offers, we are incorporated into God's family (an everlasting kingdom of love) and called to live in complete unity with all of God's children in the overflow of God's love—by loving God and other people. After receiving God's amazing love for him, John Newton began to love other people as never before—including the slaves he had formerly treated as sub-human property. This chapter shows how desperately we need to absorb in the depths of our souls the heart-penetrating, mind-boggling, life-transforming love of God in Christ!

The story of the first two chapters is that we can easily slip into misunderstandings of God's judgment. We can mistakenly declare "thus judgeth the Lord" when God has not declared it (chapter one), and we can mistakenly believe that God is a heavenly bully who relishes the thought of judging us but does not love us (chapter two). When we misunderstand God's judgment, it is serious business, soul-threatening business.

Equally serious though, are misunderstandings of God's love that fail to account for the reality of his judgment. As we will see in the next chapter, belief in a God who "loves but does not judge" is more common today than belief in a God who "judges but does not love" (young Luther's problem). The image of God as only love with no judgment is appealing to hundreds of millions in our world. Though it appears to be an attractive idea, the pages ahead show why this image of God is an extremely dangerous error.

Questions for Reflection and Discussion

1. Which aspects of *Luther's life story* intrigue you the most? Explain.

2. In what ways have your parents or caretakers (by their teaching and actions) influenced your view of God, *for good or for bad*?

3. List the struggles people face when they picture God as a judge who does not love them.

4. What strikes you the most about *Jesus' teachings on love and his life of love*?

5. How does *God's amazing grace toward John Newton* inspire or encourage you?

6. What has *helped* or *hindered you* from knowing God's love in Christ at a deep level?

PART TWO

Love without Judgment

3

Image is Everything

Pictures of God in our Minds and in the New Testament

THE POWER OF IMAGES

ADVERTISING AND MODELING AGENCIES rely on it to push their services. It is on the forefront of most politicians' minds. The phrase pervades our pop culture and yields tons of Google hits. "Image is everything."

Most of us know that companies shamelessly use images to entice us to purchase their (often unneeded) products. On one level, the slogan "image is everything" tells the sad tale of how often style triumphs over substance. Do we really believe that the model comes with the rental car? On another level, however, this phrase helpfully alerts us to the profound power of images.

Images are the bread and butter of advertising precisely because, as one cultural analyst says, "they offer us something we seek—happiness, nourishment, desirability, glamour, security, power, love, fellowship, social status, health, divine presence, refuge from the muddle of daily life, a lost past, a better future."[1] Images will probably become an even more dominant part of future advertising campaigns as we shift from a hard print culture focused on written words to an electronic culture that employs a heavy dose of icons. Why bother with the word "Nike" when the swoosh logo communicates it all?

Beyond their use in current advertising, for thousands of years images have played a central role in religious life. A particularly telling point for American Christians is the way Jesus has been portrayed in our art

1. Morgan, *Lure of Images*, 2.

49

and literature. Since there is no physical description of Jesus in the Bible or early Christian history, images of Jesus are our own projections. They function as theological Rorschach (ink blot) tests where the images in our minds often say more about us than Jesus himself. Early twentieth-century public relations pioneer Bruce Barton protested against the "soft-faced and effeminate" Jesus, and instead portrayed Jesus as "a young man glowing with physical strength." In his imagination, the cleansing of the temple displayed Jesus' physical superiority over all challengers. No one would have dared enter the ultimate fighting cage with Barton's Jesus! He put it this way:

> As that lash of cords was lifted and swept over their faces or across their necks, the loose sleeve of His garment fell back to reveal a forearm on which the muscles stood out like knots of iron; against such an arm and such a shoulder there was not one among the flabby multitude who cared to risk himself.[2]

A half-century later, Miami Dolphins' lineman Norm Evans crafted a similar image of Jesus as a big, tough football star.

> I guarantee you, Christ would be the toughest guy who ever played this game.... Jesus was a real man, all right. If He were alive today, I would picture Him as a six-foot, six-inch, 260-pound defensive tackle who would always make the big plays.... Anytime you were up against Him, you'd know you were in for a long afternoon. He would be an aggressive and tremendous competitor.... I have no doubt He could play in the National Football League.... Yes, He would make it with the Miami Dolphins today and He would be a star in this league.[3]

Based on door sizes and other archeological clues, historians estimate that most Palestinian Jews in the first century were closer to five feet in height, but this seems to have little effect on our images of Jesus. Philip Yancey speaks for most of us in saying, "we prefer a tall, handsome, and, above all, slender Jesus."[4] In hindsight we can see that many of our images of Jesus have been fanciful projections. We know that we have gone wrong

---

2. See Barton, *A Young Man's Jesus*, ix, xii, and 18. Barton's vivid imagination notwithstanding, the Bible itself says nothing about Jesus striking people with a whip.

3. Norm Evans, *On God's Squad*, 181–82.

4. Yancey, *Jesus I Never Knew*, 87.

in the past. What about our more recent images of God? What do they tell us?

IMAGES OF GOD OVER THE PAST FEW DECADES IN AMERICA

With nearly seven billion people on the face of the planet, we cannot say precisely how "people today" picture God. But we can say that according to international comparisons, Americans believe in traditional Christian doctrines (God, afterlife, Bible, devil, hell, heaven, and miracles) more than people in other countries. This is especially true when Americans are compared with Europeans.[5] By world standards, Americans are the most likely to hold traditional Christian beliefs. But, exactly what do Americans believe? Recent research tells us that approximately ninety percent of Americans believe in God, with the other ten percent agnostics or atheists. This confirms *that* most Americans believe in God, but it does not tell us anything specific concerning *how* they picture this God. Precisely what images of God are the most common among Americans in recent decades?

In the 1980s the National Opinion Research Center polled representative adult Americans, with nearly 1,600 responses. They found that the image of God most likely to come to people's mind was creator (eighty-two percent). The image of God as judge was much less frequent (forty-seven percent overall), especially among college-educated respondents (thirty-four percent).[6] So, nearly all Americans believe in God as creator, but most Americans, especially those who are college-educated, do not readily picture the God in whom they believe to be a judge.

A related study in the early 1990s with University of Washington students also yielded fascinating results. When asked how *they* would *personally* describe God, seventy-nine percent of the students said God is loving, but only forty-four percent said God is a judge.[7] This finding fits

---

5. Results of International Social Survey Program, retrieved from www.religioustolerance.org. A comparison with the European Values Survey is summarized helpfully in Walter, *Eclipse of Eternity*, 32–3. Another key study is Van Der Lans, "Empirical Research into the Human Images of God," 347–60. See also Ziebertz (ed.), *Imagining God*.

6. Roof and Roof, "Review of the Polls: Images of God among Americans," 201–5. Results were similar in 1984—the last time the question was included in the General Social Survey.

7. Foster and Keating, "Measuring Androcentrism in the Western God-Concept," 366–75.

with other research from the late 1990s that found most people prefer the image of God as a nurturer over the image of God as a judge.[8]

The most extensive data on Americans' images of God in the twenty-first century comes from the Baylor Religion Survey completed in 2005, with more than 1,700 respondents. Table 1 (the most-chosen words for describing God) and Table 2 (the least-chosen words for describing God) summarize the results.[9] People's responses tell an intriguing story. In our heart of hearts, what do we Americans really think God is like?

TABLE 1: *Most-Chosen* Words That Describe God Very Well or Somewhat Well

Forgiving	Ever-Present	Loving	Kind	Just
85.6%	85.4%	84.6%	82.0%	81.9%

TABLE 2: *Least-Chosen* Words That Describe God Very Well or Somewhat Well

Punishing	Wrathful	Critical	Severe	Distant
34.4%	27.2%	25.3%	23.3%	17.1%

Once again, we see that Americans today are much more likely to hold nurturing images of God (as forgiving and loving) than judging images of God (as punishing and wrathful). Putting all this research together, *most of us are likely to describe God as loving* (approximately eight out of ten people). By contrast, *less than half of us are likely to describe God as a judge* (approximately four out of ten people). The image of God as judge is even less frequent for those who are college-educated (approximately three out of ten people). Relatively few Americans (approximately three out of ten people) believe that God is punishing, wrathful, or critical.

The bottom line is that many people picture God as loving but not judging. The popularity of nurturing, positive images of God may explain why Americans report that when they die, most think they will go to heaven (sixty-four percent), while less than one percent think they will go

8. Krejci, "Gender Comparison of God Schemas," 57–66. See also Kunkel et. al., "God Images: A Concept Map," 193–202. These studies with adults can be contrasted with the massive survey of American adolescents in 2002–2003 that found among teens between the ages of thirteen and seventeen, seventy-one percent say they believe "in a judgment day when God will reward some and punish others" (Smith and Denton, *Soul Searching*, 41).

9. Baylor University, *Baylor Religion Survey*, question 23 (items 67–82).

to hell.[10] We do not like to think of God as a judge and we certainly do not like to think that we will be on the wrong end of God's final judgment!

Up to this point, we have looked at society-wide surveys of all Americans. What about when we zoom in specifically on American churches? We find that the dislike for thinking of God as a judge is not restricted to national polls but is present in many pulpits as well.

GOD'S JUDGMENT (OR LACK THEREOF) IN CONTEMPORARY PREACHING

Anecdotal comments suggest that in many church circles God is rarely, if ever, proclaimed as judge. Pastor Paul Thomas observed, "Past generations of preachers almost licked their lips when it came to the subject of judgment; today, by contrast, we might be lucky if they would even open their lips on the subject." Thomas himself confesses, "when I gave a sermon on that theme last year I realized that it was the first I had ever devoted solely to the subject in thirteen years of ministry."[11] And Thomas is not alone in his hesitancy to preach God's judgment. It is a virtual epidemic among pastors.

There are several possible explanations for the decline in Christian preaching on divine judgment. One view is that most people do not think of God as a judge; so many preachers are hesitant to speak about a topic that is so foreign to their listeners. Another possibility is that pastors today want to avoid the excesses of past "hellfire and brimstone preaching." Or maybe preachers see judgment as a downer subject, and want to avoid depressing people at church. Whatever the reason, lots of preachers simply avoid God's judgment as off-limits in polite company. Divine judgment is not a nice thing to talk about or even think about, for many people. When we read about judgment in our Bibles, we often privately tuck that part of Scripture away in the corners of our minds, just like we might hang a piece of unwanted clothing back in the dark recesses of our closet.

If we thought of the Bible as a roadmap, judgment would qualify as an interstate highway. It runs across the pages of Scripture like the thick blue lines on a Rand McNally road atlas. In our day, however, it is the "road less spoken." Many of us would prefer to avoid the subject altogether—"I won't

10. This data, from random telephone surveys of a thousand or more Americans in 2001, 2002, and 2003, is reported at www.barna.org.

11. Thomas, "Judgment," 106.

bring it up if you don't bring it up." The difficulty for Christians is that the Scriptures bring it up all the time. Recall how I encountered judgment in ninety-five percent of my daily Bible readings and ninety-five percent of the books of the Bible. No matter how strenuous our efforts at collective denial, eventually we must come to terms with what the Scriptures say about God's judgment, including its prominent place in the preaching and beliefs of New Testament Christians. (The subject of judgment and love in Jesus' ministry is treated at length in chapter six.)

THE BOOK OF ACTS: A WINDOW INTO EARLY CHRISTIAN PREACHING ABOUT GOD AS JUDGE

Over seventy years ago, C. H. Dodd, a New Testament scholar, published a famous study of early Christian preaching. He summed up the early church's core proclamation with these words:

> The prophecies are fulfilled, and the new Age is inaugurated by the coming of Christ. He was born of the seed of David. He died according to the Scriptures, to deliver us out of the present evil age. He was buried. He rose on the third day according to the Scriptures. He is exalted at the right hand of God, as Son of God and Lord of quick and dead. *He will come again as Judge and Saviour of men.*[12]

The last sentence is striking. According to Dodd, the early church consistently preached that Christ will come again as both Judge and Savior. Is Dodd right? As we examine the evidence, we need to remember that one of Luke's purposes in writing the book of Acts was to show how the Christian message should be preached. So as he told the story of the early church, Luke included several model sermons or speeches by leaders such as Peter and Paul.[13] God's judgment plays a leading role in three of these passages.

Acts 10: Peter's Message to Those Gathered at Cornelius' House

One pivotal episode, in which we find a model sermon nested, is the narrative of Acts 10–11. Cornelius, a God-fearing Gentile, and Peter, a Jewish apostle, both experienced visions that brought them together. Cornelius was told to send for Peter, who would "bring you a message through which

12. Dodd, *Apostolic Preaching and Its Development*, 17. Italics added for emphasis. For an updated version of Dodd's thesis, see Lemcio, *Past of Jesus in the Gospels*, 115–29.

13. On this, see Witherington III, *Acts of the Apostles*, 39.

you and all your household will be saved" (Acts 11:13–14). Peter's saving message ended with these words: "He [Jesus] commanded us to preach to the people and to testify that he is the one whom God appointed as judge of the living and the dead. All the prophets testify about him that everyone who believes in him receives forgiveness of sins through his name" (10:42–43).

According to Peter, Jesus commissioned his apostles to preach that he was the crucified and risen Messiah (10:39–40), who had been appointed by God as the judge of everyone—both those who were still alive and those who had already died (10:42). Jesus Christ was the *Lord of all* (10:36), which included *judging all people* (10:42) and *offering forgiveness to all who believe in him* (10:43). Peter preached Jesus as *both judge and savior*. The two went hand in glove for Peter: it is precisely because we will be judged *for* our sin that we need a savior *from* our sin! As the book of Acts proceeds, we see that, like Peter, the apostle Paul also preached the combined message of God's holy judgment and loving salvation.

Acts 17: Paul's Message to the Athenians at the Areopagus (Mars Hill)

Many consider Paul's most famous sermon found in the book of Acts to be his address to the Athenians. Paul seemed glad for this opportunity to preach the gospel, and he ended his message, just as Peter had, by warning of God's judgment: "In the past God overlooked such ignorance, but now he commands all people everywhere to repent. For he has set a day when he will judge the world with justice by the man he has appointed. He has given proof of this to all men by raising him from the dead" (17:30–31).

Acts 17:31 spells out the details of how God has appointed the *time* of judgment, the *subjects* of judgment, the *standard* of judgment, and the *one who will preside* over the final judgment. First, Paul declared that the *day of judgment* was set. Though the exact time had not been revealed, Paul said the day of judgment was fixed and certain (God has "set a day when he will judge"). Second, Paul preached that God will judge *the world*. The judgment will extend to everyone God has created. Third, Paul declared that God will judge *with justice* or *in righteousness*. Since God will judge with perfect justice, there will be no mistakes and no arguments about God getting it wrong! Fourth, Paul said that judgment will come *by the man whom God has appointed*. God has chosen to judge the world by Jesus, whom God raised from the dead. We usually think of Jesus' resurrection in connection with the joy of Easter. Acts 17:31 says the resurrection is also God's proof that he will judge the world through Jesus. How often do we think of that?

As we back up and look at the big picture, we see that Paul "builds his address toward the announcement of the day of judgment," so that, "the conclusion (17:30–31) of all these arguments against the idolatry of the Athenians is the call to repentance in the face of impending judgment."[14] On the one hand, God wants people to seek him and reach out for him and find him (17:27). On the other hand, people need to turn away from their sin because God has set a day in the future when he will judge them (17:30–31). To avoid condemnation at the final judgment, we must repent and trust in Christ. God's coming judgment and the need to repent were core elements of Paul's gospel. For Paul, as for Peter, judgment and salvation were twin truths that should be kept together.

Acts 24: Paul's Discourse with Felix and Drusilla

A few chapters later, Luke tells the story of how Paul publicly defended himself before Governor Felix. While Paul was kept in custody, probably under house arrest, Felix often sent for him and conversed with him. In one of Paul's private meetings with Felix and Drusilla, his Jewish wife, we are given a glimpse into the content of their conversation. Paul spoke to Felix and Drusilla about four items: faith in Christ Jesus, "righteousness, self-control, and the judgment to come" (24:24–25).

First, Paul proclaimed that Jesus was the Christ, in whom one must trust. This would have been of special interest to Drusilla, who, as a Jew, was probably familiar with messianic expectations about the Christ. Second, Paul spoke of righteousness, which contrasted sharply with Felix's well-known record of harsh cruelty. Third, Paul discussed self-control—again in deliberate contrast to Felix's reputation for lust and greed. Fourth, Paul talked about *the judgment to come*. Felix and his wife needed to know that judgment was coming and how to avoid God's condemnation at the judgment. Drusilla was Felix's third wife, and Drusilla herself had left her husband in order to marry Felix. From Paul's perspective, this powerful couple "must face the bad news of their lost spiritual condition before they can grasp and embrace the good news."[15]

14. Hansen, "Preaching and Defence of Paul," 315, 317.

15. Larkin, *Acts*, 343.

In response to Paul's message, Felix became frightened and abruptly cut off the conversation (24:25). When things got too personal, Felix called it a day. In Felix style, when the topic of judgment comes up, many of us also change the subject. Most Christians do not like talking about judgment with each other, let alone with unbelievers. The key point here is Paul preached God's judgment and the way to escape condemnation by faith in Jesus. Paul did not shy away from speaking about God's judgment, even when his life was on the line. He was a faithful ambassador of the message Jesus gave to him.

Summary of Lessons from Early Christian Preaching in Acts

As we look back over the book of Acts, we see that Dodd was right to identify God's judgment and God's salvation as crucial components of early Christian preaching. The apostles proclaimed that God's judgment was coming, but people could be saved by repenting of their sins and trusting in Jesus. There was a consistent message—whether Peter addressed a gathering of Cornelius' Gentile family (Acts 10), or Paul conversed with a group of pagan philosophers (Acts 17), or Paul spoke to Governor Felix and his wife (Acts 24). This is not to say that God's judgment was mentioned explicitly in all the speeches of Acts, especially when addressing Jewish audiences who probably would have taken this aspect of God's character for granted (see Acts 2, 3, 13, 22). Nonetheless, the apostles included *judgment and salvation* when they preached the core Christian message to those who might not otherwise have been well acquainted with these tenets of the faith.

What gave these early Christians the courage to preach God's coming judgment, even when those Christians' lives were in the balance? Part of the answer is they were fully convinced that God's judgment was for real. Unlike many today (less than half of all Americans, according to recent polls), believers within the early church pictured God as *both judging and loving*. They did not waver in *preaching* God's judgment because they did not waver in *believing* it was true. God's judgment was a core part of early Christian *preaching* because it was also a core part of early Christian *teaching*—one of the basic tenets of the faith that all Christians were expected to believe.

ROMANS 2: A WINDOW INTO EARLY CHRISTIAN TEACHING ABOUT GOD AS JUDGE

The apostle Paul believed in God's judgment and taught it to fellow Christians in his letters. Consider Paul's letter to the Romans. After the introduction (1:1–17), Paul argues that everyone, Jew and Gentile alike, has fallen short of God's glory (1:18–3:20). More alarmingly, he says, God's wrath is being revealed against the wrongdoing of those who deliberately reject the knowledge of God available to them (1:18–32). God gives such people over to their sinful desires (1:24–31). But when we pass judgment on others, Paul says, we condemn ourselves, since we do wrong things just as they do (2:1). While God's judgment is based on truth, it is presumptuous for us to pass judgment on fellow humans, while thinking that we ourselves will escape God's judgment (2:2–3).

When our hearts are stubborn and unrepentant, Paul says, we are actually "storing up wrath against ourselves for the day of God's wrath, when his righteous judgment will be revealed" (2:5). There are many things I'd like to store up for the afterlife, but wrath is not one of them! Paul continues by saying that evildoers who reject the truth and persist in sin will face wrath and anger, while the righteous who do good and obey the Law will receive eternal life (2:7–13). Put simply, God's "wrath awaits those who reject him and do evil, but life awaits those who respond in obedience, and this granting of life has its foundation in the death of Christ."[16] God's judgment will be impartial—whether to Jews who have the written Law or to Gentiles who have the requirements of the Law written internally on their hearts (2:11–15). Everyone will be judged justly in the end.

Romans 2 is packed with a theology of judgment, which all leads up to Romans 2:16, in which Paul says, "this will take place on the day when God will judge men's secrets through Jesus Christ, as my gospel declares." This verse is startling because Paul here asserts that his gospel (the gospel given to him through a revelation of Jesus Christ) includes the proclamation that some day God will judge people's secrets through Jesus Christ.

---

16. Snodgrass, "Justification by Grace—to the Doers," 82. Yinger's study of Paul concurs that "those who had already been justified by grace through faith in Christ were expected (by God's grace and the Holy Spirit, of course) to live righteous lives as well. That is, their righteousness by faith would manifest itself in obedience, in works; though not necessarily in sinless perfection. . . . The eschatological recompense according to deeds *confirms*, on the basis of deeds, one's justification" (*Paul, Judaism, and Judgment According to Deeds*, 290, italics original).

Judgment is part of Paul's gospel! The judgment will be penetrating. It will search out our formerly hidden secrets, uncovering what has been kept from other people.

Everything, including our private thoughts and internal motives, will be laid bare before God on that coming day of judgment. That is a sobering thought, but it is matched with a comforting thought for Christ's followers. God the Father will judge, but he will judge *through* Jesus Christ. Since God's judgment is carried out by Jesus—the very one who died to save his followers—they need not fear the outcome. As Paul will say later in this letter, "there is now therefore no condemnation for those who are in Christ Jesus" (8:1). The good news is that all who are "in Christ" (all who believe in Jesus and follow him as Lord and Savior) will be delivered from condemnation at the final judgment!

Emphasizing this point, one church leader observed that, "God's judgment is part of the gospel" and "we cheapen the gospel if we represent it as a deliverance only from unhappiness, fear, guilt and other felt needs, instead of as a rescue from the coming wrath."[17] The gospel is not just a pitch for personal self-improvement. Paul's gospel, his message of good news, proclaimed that a day is coming when God will judge our secrets through Jesus. The fact that God's judgment is coming (Romans 2) impresses on us the need to be delivered from judgment through faith in Jesus' saving death (Romans 3–4).

All sin must be judged, either in Christ or in ourselves. That is probably why Paul talked about God's judgment so much. If we are willing to listen to the message of God's judgment, it can sober us up in a good way . . . sort of like when doctors tell us we have to make changes in our lifestyles or we will be dead in just a few years. It is the tough message we need to hear when we are heading down a fatal path. And these warnings of God's judgment were not something unique to Paul. As the next section shows, God's judgment is also a theme that echoes again and again throughout the book of Hebrews.

HEBREWS 6: ANOTHER WINDOW INTO EARLY CHRISTIAN TEACHING ABOUT GOD AS JUDGE

The book of Hebrews was addressed to people who were in danger of "shrinking back" (10:39) from the Christian community in hopes of a

17. Stott, *Romans*, 88.

more favorable judgment from non-Christian society. It may be written to Jewish believers in Jesus, though we cannot identify the intended audience with certainty.[18] What we know for sure is that the book is saturated with concern that the readers not drift away from the faith they had embraced (2:1–3, 3:7—4:13, 5:11—6:12, 10:19–39, 12:14–29), and for which they had formerly suffered hostility and persecution (10:32–34). So Hebrews is a book full of warnings.

Early on, the author reminds the readers that, "nothing in all creation is hidden from God's sight. Everything is uncovered and laid bare before the eyes of him to whom we must give account" (4:13). There is no hiding from God. Whether it is our thoughts or words or deeds, God sees all the good and all the bad in us that no one else notices. Later the author warns that, "if we deliberately keep on sinning after we have received the knowledge of the truth, no sacrifice for sins is left, but only a fearful expectation of *judgment* and of raging fire that will consume the enemies of God" (10:26–27).

The writer reinforces this theme by stating that, "the Lord will *judge* his people" (10:30), immediately before warning them that, "it is a dreadful thing to fall into the hands of the living God" (10:31). A bit later, the author calls the readers to worship God acceptably, with reverence and awe, since "our God is a consuming fire" (12:28–29). Marital purity is also required for God's holy people, the author insists, because "God will *judge* the adulterer and all the sexually immoral" (13:4). If we thought Paul was beating the drum of God's judgment loudly in his letter to the Romans, a quick survey of Hebrews shows us that the author of this book has cranked it up several decibels!

Given such an understanding of God as judge, it is not surprising that the author considers "eternal judgment" to be among the elementary teachings of the faith—the basics that any young believer should master before moving on to deeper matters. The writer seems grieved or aggravated that his readers are "slow to learn" (5:11) and "need someone to teach you the elementary truths of God's word all over again" (5:12). By this time they should have advanced to solid food suited for mature people, but

---

18. Bruce, *Epistle to the Hebrews*, 8–9. Lane observes uncertainties on "the identity of the writer, his conceptual background, the character and location of the community addressed, the circumstances and date of composition, the setting in life, the nature of the crisis to which the document is a response, the literary genre, and the purpose and plan of the work" (*Word Biblical Commentary: Hebrews 1–8*, xlvii).

sadly they still needed the infant's milk of the basics (5:12—5:14). All this background helps us to make sense of the exhortation found in Hebrews 6:1–2: "Therefore let us leave the elementary teachings about Christ and go on to maturity, not laying again the foundation of repentance from acts that lead to death, and of faith in God, instruction about baptisms, the laying on of hands, the resurrection of the dead, and *eternal judgment*."

It may surprise our twenty-first-century ears to hear that *eternal judgment* is one of the "elementary truths of God's word" (5:12), "elementary teachings about Christ" (6:1), or half-dozen foundational elements that should be mastered by beginners in the faith (5:12—6:2). Eternal judgment is something we should have learned as kindergarten Christians, according to the author of Hebrews. It is a fundamental building block of the faith. Just like we should expect kindergartners to know their ABCs, we should expect Christians to know about eternal judgment and to live with that reality in mind.

The exhortation of Hebrews is strong, telling its original readers (and us today!) that God's judgment is eternal, everlasting, never to be changed. That is why we should have a healthy respect for God's judgment. Hebrews tells us to worry more about what God thinks than what the world around us thinks. In the end, people's judgments will not really matter since ultimately we will all stand before God for *eternal judgment*.

DANGERS OF MAKING GOD IN OUR IMAGE

A widely circulated quote says that "in the beginning God made man in his own image, and ever since man has returned the favor."[19] Looking back over this chapter, it is hard to deny that in our world today we often picture God in ways that have drifted pretty far from what is revealed about God in the New Testament. International comparisons show that Americans hold traditional Christian beliefs about God more than people in other countries. But while ninety percent of Americans say they believe in God, recent polls show that often we have fashioned a God of our own making, ignoring his judgment.

The good news is that most of us rightly understand that God is a forgiving, ever-present, loving, kind creator. The bad news is that most of us do not understand that God is also a wrathful judge who punishes sin. For the author to the Hebrews, eternal judgment was one of the six

19. Variations of this quote have been attributed to Pascal, Voltaire, and Dostoevsky.

foundational teachings of Christ. For the apostle Paul, God's judgment was part of his very gospel. The early Christians preached God's judgment as part of their core message, reflected in the book of Acts. Clearly, God's judgment is something that Jesus' followers should believe and proclaim to others.

But still we might wonder, is this really that big of a deal? Maybe downplaying God's judgment is a good thing because it keeps us from turning people off to God and reminds us not to be judgmental—thinking we are better than others. Is anything valuable actually lost when God's judgment is not believed or preached as it once was by the New Testament church? Does this part of Christian teaching and preaching (or its absence) truly affect our lives in any concrete ways? The final pages of this chapter make the case that it does matter. What we believe (or fail to believe) about God's judgment can make a huge difference in three major areas of life: ethics, evangelism, and theology.

JUDGMENT AND ETHICS

When we are convinced of God's judgment, as taught in the Bible, it can serve as a powerful incentive to believe and live righteously. The author of Hebrews, as noted earlier, holds out the fear of God's eternal judgment as an incentive for living godly lives. On the flip side, many New Testament passages set forth the hope of rewards in eternity as a reason to obey and please God.[20] (We do not obey in order to earn a place in heaven, but pursue treasure in heaven as those saved by God's grace.[21]) The eternal consequence of God's judgment is like a compass that helps orient our moral maps in this world. By contrast, much contemporary thinking promotes an "ethics without eternity."[22]

Think about how strange an "ethics without eternity" would have sounded to the apostle Peter. The book we know as 1 Peter draws a close connection between God's judgment and our ethics—how we should live. Peter exhorted believers, who had been redeemed by Christ's blood, to live in reverent fear during the time of their stay on earth since they "call on a Father who *judges* each one's work impartially" (1:17–19). Peter said *judg-*

---

20. Luke 14:12–4; 2 Corinthians 5:9–10; 1 Timothy 6:18–9.

21. Luke 12:32–3; 1 Corinthians 3:5–15; Ephesians 2:8–10.

22. Walter, *Eclipse of Eternity*, 1. A few pages later, Walter observes, "how unusual modern western societies are in being oriented only to this world" (3).

ment will begin first with the family of God, and will also extend to ungodly sinners who do not obey the gospel of God (4:17–18). Unbelievers who continually yield to their sinful desires, "will have to give account to him who is ready to *judge* the living and the dead" (4:5). Peter proclaimed God's coming judgment as a key motivator for people to repent and live godly lives. Our daily ethics, Peter said, should be shaped by the fact that God will judge us and hold us accountable for our lives.

The basic idea behind moral accountability is common sense to most of us. People live differently when they believe they will not be held accountable for their actions. When there is no deadline to meet, report to file, or monthly sales incentive, workers often do less on the job. If they sense no police are around, people speed more. If they think no one will find out, people are more likely to look at internet pornography. Conversely, when we are held accountable, most of us tend to behave more responsibly.

This principle of moral accountability connects with our beliefs about God's judgment in two obvious ways. (1) If we believe that God really judges, then we will want to avoid God's eternal condemnation— "negative motivation" to believe and live rightly. As the author of the book of Hebrews says, since God sees everything and we must give account of ourselves to God, we should "hold firmly to the faith we profess" (4:13–14). (2) If we believe that God really judges, then we will want to please God and receive God's gracious reward—"positive motivation" to believe and live rightly. Again, according to the book of Hebrews, if you "do not throw away your confidence, it will be richly rewarded. You need to persevere so that when you have done the will of God, you will receive what he has promised" (10:35–36). Whether we seek to avoid God's terrifying condemnation or seek to receive God's gracious reward, God's judgment can have a profound impact on our day-to-day lives. When we cease to believe in God's judgment, we lose an important biblical motivation for living ethically.[23]

Psalm 115 describes nations that do not revere the true God of Israel but instead worship handmade idols of silver and gold. The Psalmist

---

23. While God's judgment is admittedly one among many biblical motivations for living ethically, it is an important motivation that is lost to many today. As I have argued elsewhere, "it is characteristic of New Testament paranaesis or moral exhortation to present people with multiple reasons to do the right thing, without devaluing any of these reasons" (Moroney, "Higher Stages?" 369).

mocks these lifeless idols and says of them that "those who make them will be like them, and so will all who trust in them." Hence the saying, "we become like what we worship."[24] Think about that. When we cease to worship a God who judges right and wrong by a perfect standard of justice, we may find ourselves less willing and less able to exercise moral judgment. If God does not judge, how are we to discern the difference between good and evil in this world? Without a God who judges right and wrong and who reveals his standards to us, we are set adrift on a sea of relativism, wandering without a sure moral compass. So, belief in God's judgment can make a profound difference in how we live our lives.

JUDGMENT AND EVANGELISM

Beyond its effect on our ethics, if Christians today weaken our belief in God's judgment and do not proclaim it to others, our evangelistic message will be diminished. As one theologian put it, "the Christian witness must learn how to declare a judgment to come in terms that make sense. Unless this happens, repentance will be impossible and the salvation rescue will appear unnecessary and hence irrelevant."[25] This claim may overstate the case for dramatic effect. After all, some biblical presentations of the gospel, leading to repentance and faith, do not explicitly mention judgment (Acts 2, 3, and 16). Still, judgment is an important component of many gospel presentations summarized in Scripture. We must admit that "the Bible offers ample evidence that one of the ways to present the gospel to powerful people is to confront them with the reality of judgment."[26]

Christians are called to represent Christ since we are "Christ's ambassadors" or "those who have been approved by God to be entrusted with the gospel."[27] The main job of ambassadors is to be faithful messengers of those whom they represent. In one church leader's words, "the scary thing is that while it is true that God speaks for God, in a real sense we as Christians speak for God."[28] When Christians today depart from the early church's core gospel message by muting or removing God's judgment from our evangelism, we are in real danger of misrepresenting the

24. See Beale, *We Become What We Worship*.

25. Larkin, *Acts*, 344.

26. Fernando, *Acts*, 586.

27. 2 Corinthians 5:20 and 1 Thessalonians 2:4.

28. Tucker, *God Talk*, 31.

one for whom we speak. The judgment to come is part of God's message entrusted to us. As Christ's messengers, we are not at liberty to change the message by hitting the delete button on God's judgment.

Paul famously declared in Romans 1:16: "I am not ashamed of the gospel, because it is the power of God for the salvation of everyone who believes: first for the Jew, then for the Gentile." A chapter later, Paul explained that his gospel included the fact that one day God will judge people's secrets through Jesus Christ (2:16). That is bad news since we are all sinners who have fallen short of God's glory. But the good news is we can be justified or declared righteous by God's grace, through the redemption that is in Jesus (3:23–24). Believing the bad news that God judges our sin naturally precedes believing the good news that Jesus has borne God's judgment in the place of sinners.

As recent financial crises have taught us all too painfully, people do not really worry about their debts unless they realize that eventually they will have to account for them. If God never judges our sin, then there is no wrath from which we need to be saved. As one theologian said, "to realize that we are under God's wrath and in dis-grace is the essential preliminary to the experience of His love and His grace. In this respect the Christian gospel is bad news before it is good news."[29]

Sometimes we are tempted to think that our evangelistic outreach will be hurt if we include the part about God judging sin. We may tell ourselves that people are already down enough and don't want to hear any more bad news. But, in contrast to this mindset, Paul shows us it is best to keep the twin truths of judgment and salvation together, when he says in Romans 3:26 that God is "just and the one who justifies those who have faith in Jesus." Because God is just he will judge sin, but because God is loving he has provided a way for people to be justified (legally declared as righteous) by faith in Jesus.

Once the foundation of God's judgment has been set, we really appreciate what Jesus has done for us. As Paul said in Romans 5:9: "Since we have now been justified by his blood, how much more shall we be saved from God's wrath through him!" If we do not believe that Jesus came to rescue us from God's wrath, we will not be fully equipped or fully motivated to proclaim this good news to others. One author put it this way:

29. Tasker, *Biblical Doctrine of the Wrath of God*, 8.

The grace that is truly amazing is a grace that first causes hearts to fear and then brings relief—not one that persuades them that there was never anything to be afraid of in the first place. The love of Christ as expressed in His death on the cross is a love that is inevitably misunderstood until it is seen against the backdrop of the crushing issues of sin, wrath, hell, and divine sovereignty.[30]

JUDGMENT AND THEOLOGY

The final area at stake is the most obvious, the most basic, and in some ways the most important. It has to do with what we believe about God. If, as recent polls tell us, many of us hold to an image of God as one who loves but does not judge, then we will have a weakened and distorted understanding of who God is. Our theology will be diminished. And that is serious business. One church leader put it this way:

> The gravest question before the Church is always God Himself, and the most portentous fact about any person is not what he at a given time may say or do, but what he in his deep heart conceives God to be like. We tend by a secret law of the soul to move toward our mental image of God. This is true not only of the individual Christian, but of the company of Christians that composes the Church. Always the most revealing thing about the Church is her idea of God, just as her most significant message is what she says about God or leaves unsaid.... So necessary to the Church is a lofty concept of God that when that concept in any measure declines, the Church with her worship and her moral standards declines along with it. The first step down for any church is taken when it surrenders its high opinion of God.[31]

As many thinkers have observed over the years, what we believe affects how we live.[32] Adolf Hitler's ideas about the supremacy of the Aryan race were catastrophic for millions upon millions. Karl Marx's ideas about economics and God ("the opiate of the masses") have influenced the daily lives of billions. Many lives today are shaped by the idea that there is no

30. Clotfelter, *Sinners in the Hands of a Good God*, 20.

31. Tozer, *Knowledge of the Holy*, 9, 12.

32. Regardless of whether all his examples are convincing, the general point is made by Weaver, *Ideas Have Consequences*. On a more popular level, see Sproul, *Consequences of Ideas*. We must acknowledge, however, that how we behave also influences what we believe—as in the phenomenon of rationalization. The flow between behavior and belief is bidirectional.

ultimate truth in the universe and that the best we can hope for is to create our own truths—either individually or collectively. Of course, the very idea of judgment requires a prior belief that there is such a thing as right and wrong in the universe. If there is no ultimate standard of right and wrong, there can be no judgment. And the idea that there will be no final judgment can shape us in powerful ways.

Psalm 10 describes a wicked person. It tells us of his wicked actions: hunting down the weak, devising schemes, ambushing victims, and speaking boasts, curses, lies, and threats. It also tells us of his theology. He reviles the Lord and does not seek God. He says to himself that God has forgotten, never sees what is going on, and will not call him to account. In short, the wicked person has no fear of God's judgment, and this emboldens his wicked actions. The connection within Psalm 10 is clear: a wrong idea about God (denying that God sees and judges) is associated with evil behavior.

The same point is made in the New Testament in the book of 2 Peter, chapter 3. People who follow their own evil desires are described as foolishly scoffing at Jesus' promise to come again. They tell themselves that everything goes on as it has since the beginning of creation. They believe they will never be held accountable for their actions, so they can pursue their evil desires without fear of future judgment. According to Peter, however, these wicked scoffers have a faulty theology. First, they deliberately forget that God is a judge. The same God who judged the world by a flood in the past will also judge ungodly people with a fire in the future. Second, they fail to understand that God does not view time as we do. Though it may seem that God is slow to keep the promise of Christ's second coming, actually God is showing patience in providing plenty of time for people to come to repentance. Again, bad theology is associated with bad living. What we believe (or fail to believe) about God's judgment really matters!

CONCLUSION

Whether in advertising or in religion, the popular slogan "image is everything" alerts us to the profound power of images in our lives, for good or bad. Research shows that, on the whole, Americans embrace more traditional Christian images of God than people in other countries. Yet, these same Americans who quickly embrace images of God as nurturing are slow to embrace images of God as judging. Many preachers today also admit they are slow to preach God's judgment. This trend is a deviation from early Christian preaching and teaching about God as judge, reflected in the New Testament.

It is dangerous for us to make God in our own image rather than receiving what is revealed about God in Scripture. When we neglect God's judgment, it can have a detrimental influence on our ethics, our evangelism, and our theology. God is revealed in Scripture as, among many other things, a judge who is wrathful in response to human sin. From early in the pages of Genesis, when Abraham addresses the Lord as "the Judge of all the earth" (18:25) to late in the pages of Revelation where the great multitude in heaven sings praises to God, "for true and just are his judgments" (19:2), nearly every book in the Bible (over ninety-five percent of them) reinforces the picture of God as judge. Clearly, the image of God as judge is a vital piece of a full, biblical understanding of God's character.

The story of this chapter has been the way many people today, in society and even in church, focus too little on the biblical image of God as judge. God's judgment is an uncomfortable subject that many of us would rather avoid. In fact, some have suggested the church should dispense altogether with the idea that God is a judge. Maybe it would be more appealing just to believe in a God of love who is never wrathful in judging sin. The next chapter tells the story of famous religious leaders who have followed this path.

Questions for Reflection and Discussion

1. When you think of God, what images are most likely to come to your mind?

2. Pretend you are a participant in the Baylor Religion Survey. Circle the words that you think describe God very well or somewhat well. What Scriptures support them?

   a. absolute   i. kind
   b. critical   j. kingly
   c. distant   k. loving
   d. ever-present   l. motherly
   e. fatherly   m. punishing
   f. forgiving   n. severe
   g. friendly   o. wrathful
   h. just   p. yielding

3. When is the last time you heard a sermon on judgment? What did the minister say?

4. Should we include God's judgment when we share the gospel with people today? If so, how can we explain God's judgment in a faithful way in the context of our culture?

5. In practical terms, how do your beliefs about God's judgment affect the way you live?

4

All You Need is Love

Dangers of the Marcion Invasion and Liberal Theology

BEWARE OF THE MARCION INVASION!

THE MOST FAMOUS RADIO drama of all time is Orson Welles' "War of the Worlds." It was broadcast by CBS Radio as a pre-Halloween special on October 30, 1938, and it continues to intrigue people today. Adapting the storyline of H. G. Wells' science fiction novel by the same name, the radio production repeatedly used simulated news bulletins ("we interrupt this program . . .") to suggest that Martians were actually invading New Jersey and New York with deadly ray guns. Despite disclaimers at the beginning, middle, and end of the hour, thousands of listeners panicked, and perhaps as many as a million people were confused about whether the alleged Martian invasion was real.[1]

Similar confusion struck the Christian church in the middle of the second century with "the Marcion invasion." According to church leaders of the time, around 140 AD/CE, a wealthy ship builder named Marcion burst onto the scene in Rome, offering the church a huge financial gift. At first Marcion was received warmly, but as time wore on, serious concerns arose about his teaching. In the year 144, church leaders in Rome called an official meeting to determine what to do about Marcion and the ideas he was spreading. The church decided to excommunicate Marcion (or he left on his own, some say). The church also took up a speedy collection to return every penny of his earlier gift. That doesn't happen every day. So, what was the problem with Marcion's teaching?

---

1. See Dunning, *On the Air*; Hand, *Terror on the Air!*; and Nachman, *Raised on Radio*.

To begin with, Marcion taught the existence of two different Gods—one revealed in Judaism and the other in Christianity. Marcion saw Christianity as a completely new religion that was disconnected from Judaism. In his view, Jesus was not the promised Messiah who was prophesied in the Hebrew Scriptures. Rather, Jesus revealed to people the highest God who was previously unknown—the God of love. Marcion said that the inferior God of the old covenant wrathfully judged people for their sins, whereas the superior God of the new covenant lovingly forgave people of their sins.

So, Marcion said, Christians should reject the Hebrew Scriptures altogether. His "Bible" consisted of part of Luke's gospel, followed by ten of Paul's letters—all of which were edited in accordance with his beliefs. Marcion's Scriptures left out references to God's judgment, wrath, or punishment of sin. In his view, the good God of Christianity loves everyone and never punishes sinners, not even in a final judgment.

Marcion also had an unusual outlook on Jesus. In his scheme, Christ "did not come in real flesh, he did not suffer, and he did not die or rise in the flesh."[2] Marcion did not believe that people were guilty before a holy God or that Jesus died as an atonement for people's sins. So, if his view was accepted, "the call to repent, the imminence of judgment, fear and trembling, atonement—all these are eliminated from the Christian message."[3] Regrettably, thousands followed Marcion's religion, which remained popular, even after his break with the church at Rome. Not surprisingly, pastors and theologians of the time believed it was urgent that they respond to Marcion's ideas.

THE EARLY CHURCH RESPONDS
TO THE MARCION INVASION

A second-century church leader named Irenaeus argued against Marcion's teaching on "the two Gods." Irenaeus said it was a mistake to distinguish between the lesser God who judges in anger and the greater God who is good. He considered this belief in two different "Gods" a fatal flaw in

---

2. Dungan, *History of the Synoptic Problem*, 51. These points are documented, respectively, in Tertullian's *Against Marcion*, 3.8.1, 3.11.8. and 3.8.6.

3. Jonas, *Gnostic Religion*, 143.

Marcion's theology because, Irenaeus said, if there is not one God who is *both* good and a just judge, then God is not truly God.[4]

Similar reasoning peppered the writings of a church leader named Tertullian at the start of the third century. Tertullian rejected Marcion's teaching on the two Gods, and instead asserted that "God is good and severe to the same people, but at different times."[5] There were some differences in what God required in the Old Testament era and in the New Testament era, but Tertullian insisted that it was still the same God throughout.

Both Irenaeus and Tertullian said that Marcion's "good God" who never acted as a judge and never actually enforced the moral law was a deficient God. What is the use of laws if they are never put into effect? They would be just empty threats. The correct view, according to the early church, was that God really does judge sin, but that God also provides for the forgiveness of sin through Christ. In opposition to Marcion, Tertullian and other leaders said that God's judgment and God's love go together perfectly.[6]

Consequently, the early church declared Marcion's teachings to be heretical and warned Christians not to attend Marcionite assemblies. Within a hundred years of his death, Marcion had few followers in the western half of the Roman Empire, and by the fifth century his movement had dwindled in the east also. For the next 1500 years Marcion's teachings had minimal influence, at most.[7] It seemed that the church had successfully repelled the Marcion invasion. In the past hundred years, however, there has been a fresh revival of interest in Marcion and renewed support for his teachings.

---

4. Irenaeus, *Against Heresies*, 1.27.2, 3.25.2, 3.25.3, and 4.28.1.

5. Osborn, *Tertullian*, 89. See Tertullian, *Against Marcion*, 1.19.4–5, 4.6.1. Reproduced in Hultgren and Haggmark (eds.), *Earliest Christian Heretics*, 106–107, 111.

6. Tertullian, *Against Marcion*, 2.16.1. As May put it, Tertullian argued that "in spite of all apparent and actual differences between Old and New Testaments, one can adhere to the unity of God and to continuity of his actions" ("Marcion in Contemporary Views—Results and Open Questions," 141.) Besides what Irenaeus and Tertullian said, Marcion was also criticized by later church leaders named Hippolytus, Origen, Cyril of Jerusalem, Epiphanius, Chrysostom, and others.

7. Some speculate that Marcion's teachings influenced later dualist groups such as Manichaeans, Bogomils, and Cathars. On this, see Stoyanov, *The Other God*, 107, 162. See also Sean Martin, *The Cathars*, 28, 53.

THE GHOST OF MARCION STILL HAUNTS US TODAY

A theologian named Adolf von Harnack worked off and on for over fifty years to produce the definitive twentieth-century book on Marcion. Harnack gushed that Marcion was "my first love in church history," and argued that Marcion's "way of proclaiming the gospel remarkably addresses the needs of the present day," since "only the proclamation of a hopeful nonjudgmental love now has any prospect of being heard." Harnack wanted Christianity to return to Marcion's teaching that "*the loving will of Jesus (and, that is, of God) does not judge, but comes to our aid.*"[8] The bottom line is that Harnack wanted to revive Marcion's idea that God only loves and never judges sinners, no matter what.

Besides Harnack, other contemporary scholars have taken an interest in Marcion. In recent years Marcion has been characterized as "a pioneer in the quest for a norm of faithfulness, not the heretic he has been made out to be" and "the first in a long line of church reformers whom God has raised up to call the church to faithfulness."[9] One thinker said, "Marcion's message of the new and alien God will never fail to touch the human heart," and another asked us to pave the way for Marcion's "return home to the church."[10] And it is not just some ivory-tower scholars who are interested in Marcion.

Marcion's thinking also sways people on the popular level, insofar as the notion is "still found among Christians today, that the Old Testament God is a God of wrath, whereas the New Testament God is a God of love and mercy."[11] In the words of one analyst, Marcion's "ideas have more practical influence today than ever before," and "evangelicalism has become practically Marcionite at a number of levels"—evident in the way that "the emphasis upon God's love to the utter exclusion of everything else has become something of a commonplace."[12] For example, consider the recent bestselling book by the pastor of America's largest church con-

---

8. Harnack, *Marcion*, foreword to the first edition, 143. Italics in the original. This work was originally published in German in 1924.

9. Whether precisely accurate or not, these characterizations of John Howard Yoder's view of Marcion are found in Miller, "In the Footsteps of Marcion," 85–6.

10. Jonas, *Gnostic Religion*, 146; Lüdemann, *Heretics*, 169.

11. Ehrman, *Lost Christianities*, 252–253. See the related remark on page 107.

12. Trueman, "Marcions Have Landed!" 1.

gregation, Joel Osteen, which asserts that God "is not an angry, condemning God. He is a loving, merciful, forgiving God."[13]

Of course, few in the church these days want to exclude the Old Testament from the Bible, as Marcion did, let alone teach that Jesus reveals a different God than the Creator described in the Hebrew Scriptures. Many, however, hold to Marcion's contrast between God's wrath and judgment in the Old Testament and God's love and mercy in the New Testament. One author put it starkly:

> I can't handle this angry, vindictive God of the Old Testament, smoke pouring out of his nostrils, coals of fire spitting from his mouth. How can you expect me to go along with such barbaric primitivism? No thanks. I'll stick with Jesus. Jesus who "loves the little children, all the children of the world" and never raises his voice. You can have all that Old Testament yelling and stomping as far as I'm concerned. I'm a New Testament person. I'm a Jesus Christian.[14]

Relatives, friends, and college students in my theology courses have expressed the same perspective. This popular view of the Bible, however, cannot be sustained by the Bible itself—where we find plenty of God's love and mercy in the Old Testament and plenty of God's judgment and wrath in the New Testament. The following sections show that Marcion's view, held by many today, crumbles under the weight of biblical evidence.

---

13. Osteen, *Become a Better You*, 96. This statement is addressed indiscriminately to all readers. When asked on Larry King Live (10/17/07), "where is the fire and brimstone?" Osteen replied that, there's just "different ways to present it," and in defense of his positive approach to the gospel message he noted that, "there's a Scripture that says it's the goodness of God that leads people to repentance." Here Osteen cited Romans 2:4 in a way that confuses the source of repentance—God's goodness—with the content of the gospel message that leads people to repentance. Contextually, the preceding verses (Romans 2:1–3) speak of God's judgment and the following verses (Romans 2:5–8) speak of the day of God's wrath and God's righteous judgment—neither of which is mentioned by Osteen. This interview can be viewed as a video and is available in transcript form at http://transcripts.cnn.com/TRANSCRIPTS/0710/16/lkl.01.html.

14. Peterson, "Foreword," in Galli, *Jesus Mean and Wild*. In this passage Peterson is offering a poignant characterization of what a modern-day Marcionite might say, but Peterson is *not* endorsing this perspective.

IN THE OLD TESTAMENT, GOD SHOWS LOVE AND MERCY ALONGSIDE WRATH AND JUDGMENT

One of Marcion's key errors was that he saw *only wrath and never mercy* in the Old Testament portrayal of God. In terms of what we learned in chapter three, we might say that Marcion did not have a very full image of who God is. In his view, the Old Testament was all about God's judgment and never about God's love. However, when we actually examine famous Old Testament passages, even ones that might be considered to be mainly "judgment stories," we find clear portrayals of God's love and mercy.

God's Love and Mercy in the Early Period of the Patriarchs (Genesis, Exodus)

One of the most famous judgment stories in the Old Testament is the destruction of Sodom and Gomorrah. Theologians today debate the cause of God's judgment here. Some say that the citizens' attempt to gang rape Lot's visitors was the focus of judgment, while others argue that the real offenses were Sodom's haughty arrogance and lack of concern with helping the poor and needy.[15] Both sides agree, though, that Genesis 19 describes God as an angry judge who pours out wrathful judgment on wrong-doers—by blinding the men of the city, raining down burning sulphur on Sodom and its surrounding area, and turning Lot's wife into a pillar of salt. Even within this classic story of God's judgment of sin, however, there is an often neglected element of God's mercy.

Despite his visitors' urgent pleas for Lot and his family to exit the city speedily, we are told that Lot was hesitant to leave. Thankfully, the angels sent to display God's wrath toward Sodom's sin were also sent to display God's mercy toward Lot's family. The angels grasped the hands of Lot, his wife, and his two daughters, and led them out of the city, "for the LORD was merciful to them." God's loving mercy is found in the midst of this "judgment story." Lot himself reinforces the point, when he says to his angelic rescuers, "you have shown great kindness to me in sparing my life." Instead of leaving Lot in Sodom to be judged with the others, God mercifully sent angels to rescue Lot and his family from the destruction.

---

15. The attempted gang rape is highlighted in Genesis 19:1–11 and is reinforced by the condemnation of Sodom's sexual immorality and perversion in Jude 1:7. Haughty arrogance and unconcern with helping the poor and needy are highlighted in Ezekiel 16:49–50. Of course, it is likely that God judged all these sins.

And beyond the case of Lot, the book of Genesis tells many stories of God's loving-kindness and faithfulness to Abraham, Jacob, and Joseph.[16]

God's love and mercy, evident in the book of Genesis, are displayed even more prominently in the book of Exodus. No sooner had the covenant been confirmed on Mount Sinai than the people abandoned their loyalty to God in favor of worshipping the golden calf. God brought judgment through the Levites' swords and a plague, but God also relented mercifully from wiping out the Israelites completely. In response to Israel's betrayal, God proclaims himself to be "the LORD, the LORD, the compassionate and gracious God, slow to anger, abounding in love and faithfulness, maintaining love to thousands, and forgiving wickedness, rebellion, and sin. Yet he does not leave the guilty unpunished; he punishes the children and their children for the sin of the fathers to the third and fourth generation."[17] This self-description affirms God's punishment of sin, but as one expert said, "its nucleus proclaims Israel's God as a god of love and faithfulness" and "God's love takes the shape of faithfulness and mercy that is willing to forgive—not only once, but once and over again."[18] This God who is compassionate, gracious, and abounding in love is far removed from Marcion's Old Testament God who is only wrath.

God's Love and Mercy in the Period of the United Monarchy (2 Samuel, Psalms)

God's judgment and steadfast love remain on display, side by side, during the period of the united monarchy—when Israel was united under one king (first Saul, then David, then Solomon). Second Samuel 7 records God's gracious promise that David's descendants would experience punishment for wrongdoing, but God's love would never be taken from them. As one commentator said, "the love of God for David and his sons does not exclude judgment, but the judgment will never eclipse the love of God towards the sons of David."[19] In this way God would establish David's house, throne, and kingdom forever. David cherished God's promise of steadfast love, and sang of how the Lord "shows unfailing kindness to his

---

16. See Genesis 24:12–4, 24:27 (Abraham); 32:9–10 (Jacob); and 39:20–3 (Joseph).

17. Exodus 34:6–7.

18. Spieckermann, "God's Steadfast Love," 311–12.

19. Zachman, "Unity of Judgment and Love," 154.

anointed, to David and his descendants forever." Solomon likewise trea-
sured God's loving covenant loyalty to him.[20]

Consider also how God's judgment and love are interspersed
throughout the book of Psalms. God is pictured as the judge of the earth,
who judges his people and all the earth (50:1–7, 75:4–8, 94:1–2, 105:5–7).
More than thirty psalms contain pleas for God to carry out judgment (see
for example, 35:1–28, 109:1–20). At the same time, many psalms repeat
the description of God from Exodus 34:6–7, that the Lord is a compassionate and gracious God, slow to anger, abounding in love and faithfulness (86:15, 103:8, 145:8). The psalms exult in God's steadfast love toward
Israel collectively (103:6–18, 136:1–26) and toward David and his family
in particular (89:19–37). That is why God's steadfast love "has been regarded as the most important theological term there is to describe God's
being and acting in the realm of the Psalter's theology."[21] The emphasis on
God's steadfast love and mercy in the book of Psalms contrasts sharply
with Marcion's claims.

God's Love and Mercy in the Prophets and after the Exile (Hosea, Nehemiah)

The same is true with the prophets. Perhaps no book tells the heart-
wrenching story of God's unrequited love for Israel more poignantly than
Hosea. Just as the prophet Hosea was the husband of sexually adulterous
Gomer, God is pictured as the husband of spiritually adulterous Israel
(ch. 1). The catalog of Israel's sins is embarrassingly long and requires ten
chapters to describe (chs. 4–13). Repeatedly we are told God will judge
Israel for its wrongdoing. The land will be destroyed, many people will be
massacred, and the remainder will be exiled to wander among the nations
(chs. 5, 8, 9, 10, 13).

Still, in the end, Hosea tells a story of love rejected and love restored.
God responds to Israel's spiritual adultery with the promise of re-courting
(2:14–23). As Gomer would be redeemed by her loving husband, Hosea,
so Israel would be redeemed by her loving husband, the Lord (3:1–5).
There is a bright promise of God's re-betrothal (2:19–20) and compas-

---

20. See 2 Samuel 22, 1 Kings 3, and 1 Kings 8. The same Hebrew word *hesed* is a
constant thread in the descriptions of God's steadfast love and kindness toward Lot (Gen.
19:19), Abraham (Gen. 24:27), Isaac (Gen. 32:10), Joseph (Gen. 39:21), David (2 Sam.
7:15, 22:51), and the nation of Israel (Ex. 34:6; Ps. 98:3).

21. Spieckermann, "God's Steadfast Love," 314.

sionate mercy to the Israelites (11:8–9). God will heal their waywardness, love them freely, and cause them to blossom, grow, and flourish (14:4–8). Israel's soon-coming judgment, then, is set within the overarching story of God's persevering love, leading ultimately to Israel's restoration.

A few centuries later, when Israel was restored to the land after the exile, their leaders confessed to the Lord that "you are a forgiving God, gracious and compassionate, slow to anger and abounding in love." Their hope for the future rested in "our God, the great, mighty and awesome God, who keeps his covenant of love."[22] What a sharp contrast to Marcion's harsh, Old Testament God of wrath!

So, whether looking at the Old Testament at the beginning (Genesis and Exodus), middle (united monarchy and psalms), or end (prophets and post-exile era), the Israelites consistently portrayed God's character in multi-dimensional terms. God's justice and mercy, wrath and love, judgment and kindness appear inseparable. Marcion's dichotomy between the "Old Testament God of wrath" and "New Testament God of love" just does not work. The "Old Testament God" shows abundant love (alongside wrath), and as the next section proves, the "New Testament God" shows abundant wrath (alongside love).

IN THE NEW TESTAMENT, GOD SHOWS WRATH AND JUDGMENT ALONGSIDE LOVE AND MERCY

God's Wrath and Judgment in the Gospel of John

The Gospel of John is a favorite of many people. It was written by "the disciple whom Jesus loved" (21:20–24), and it throws a bright spotlight on God's love. It was out of love that God sent his one and only Son into the world to save it (3:16–17). John introduced Jesus' final days on earth by saying that, "having loved his own who were in the world, he now showed them the full extent of his love" (13:1). Jesus himself said that there is no greater love than for a person to lay down his life for his friends (15:13).

In the midst of this gospel of love, however, there is also a resounding witness to God's wrath and judgment. Good news and bad news even appear within the same sentence. John 3:18 says, "whoever believes in him is not condemned, *but* whoever does not believe stands condemned already because he has not believed in the name of God's one and only Son."

---

22. Nehemiah 9:17, 9:32–3.

Later in the same chapter we read that, "whoever believes in the Son has eternal life, *but* whoever rejects the Son will not see life, for God's wrath remains on him" (3:36). Wrathful condemnation and gracious eternal life come from the same God.

As John's Gospel unfolds, we read further how God lovingly provides salvation to those who believe, but also how God will judge those who do not believe. Jesus said that a time is coming when all will rise to a final judgment before the Son of Man—a judgment that seals their response to him during their lifetime—resulting in permanent life or lasting condemnation (5:24–30). So, while Jesus did not come to judge the world but to save it, at the last day those who reject him and his message will be condemned by the word he spoke from the Father (12:47–50). Unlike Marcion, John—an eyewitness to God in the flesh (1:14)—presents God's love and judgment as inextricably intertwined.

God's Wrath and Judgment in Paul's Letters (Romans, Ephesians)

We find a similar understanding of God's love and judgment in Paul's letter to the Romans. He addresses the Roman Christians as those who are "loved by God" (1:7), and he says that God's love can be seen in the way that Christ died for sinners (5:8). Those who love God and have been called according to his purpose (8:28) can rest assured, Paul says, that they are "more than conquerors through him who loved us" (8:37). There is absolutely nothing in the world that can separate them from the love of Christ (8:35–39).

But again, the emphasis on God's love is paired with a corresponding emphasis on God's wrath. On the one hand, "the righteous will live by faith" (1:17), *but* on the other hand, "the wrath of God is being revealed from heaven against all the godlessness and wickedness of men who suppress the truth by their wickedness" (1:18). Paul rejoices at how Christ's followers will "be saved from God's wrath through him" (5:9). This is especially important because "we will all stand before God's judgment seat" (14:10), when "each of us will give an account of himself to God" (14:12). In sharp divergence from Marcion, Paul's theology in Romans presents God as *both* a wrathful Judge *and* a loving Savior, *both* "just and the one who justifies those who have faith in Jesus" (3:26).

This same consistent theology is found in Paul's other letters as well. It was "in love," Paul tells the Ephesian Christians, that God "predestined us to be adopted as his sons through Jesus Christ" (1:4–5). In Christ they are forgiven, "in accordance with the riches of God's grace" (1:7). But God's love and grace are especially to be appreciated because they save us from wrath. "Like the rest we were by nature objects of wrath. But because of his great love for us, God, who is rich in mercy, made us alive with Christ even when we were dead in transgressions—it is by grace you have been saved" (2:3–5).

Later in the same letter, Paul will remind these Christians how as God's "dearly loved children" (5:1) they should avoid a whole list of ugly sins (5:3–5), "for because of such things God's wrath comes on those who are disobedient" (5:6). Whether he wrote to Rome or Ephesus, Paul affirmed *both* God's love in Christ *and* God's wrath against sin.

Summing up, the New Testament teaches that God has lovingly provided for human salvation through the Lord Jesus Christ, but those who spurn God's patient offer of forgiveness will rightly suffer the punishment they deserve. In the words of one scholar, "when the judge is the Savior who took the penalty and offered a pardon the defendants rejected, they cannot complain the verdict is unfair."[23]

God's wrathful judgment of sin and loving forgiveness in Christ are a package deal. In fact, it is the first that makes the second good news. The gospel announces God's undeserved gift to people who ought to have their sins punished. As one theologian said of Christ's death: "the event that reveals more than any other the love of God for Jews and Gentiles also reveals like no other the judgment and wrath of God against sin."[24] Contrast this with Harnack's call for the church today to proclaim only "hopeful nonjudgmental love."

Throughout the Bible, God's love and God's judgment are so intertwined they cannot be torn apart. Despite Scripture's clear teaching on this subject, Marcion's view has not died. The idea that God accepts all people without ever judging us lives vibrantly within some segments of evangelicalism, and it has been most visible within the tradition of Protestant liberalism that attempts to magnify God's love while denying God's wrath.

---

23. Keillor, *God's Judgments*, 93.
24. Zachman, "The Unity of Judgment and Love," 158.

GOD'S LOVE WITHOUT WRATH IN THE FOUNTAINHEAD
OF PROTESTANT LIBERALISM (SCHLEIERMACHER)

The most famous characterization of liberal theology is that "a God without wrath brought people without sin into a kingdom without judgment through the ministrations of a Christ without a cross."[25] As one theologian said, "it is an enduring legacy of the liberal-Protestant approach to the gospel to root out all references to God's wrath and to define God's essence as love without qualification."[26] In other words, liberal theology is very deliberate in claiming, like Marcion, that God's love and God's wrath should not be kept together. All we need is love. The intentional rejection of God's wrath is evident right from the start of liberal theology and its founding figure, Friedrich Schleiermacher.

Like many others, Schleiermacher wrote a "systematic theology"—a book that explains his teachings in all areas of doctrine. He called it *The Christian Faith*, and even though it is a hefty 750 pages, the subjects of God's wrath or judgment are referenced on just a handful of these pages. When he was discussing God's attributes, Schleiermacher did not even mention wrath, and insisted that "love alone and no other attribute can be equated thus with God." When he was discussing Christ, Schleiermacher said we can "accept Him as Redeemer or recognize the being of God in Him, [even] if we did not know that He had risen from the dead and ascended to heaven, or [even] if He had not promised that He would return for judgment." In his view, Jesus' resurrection, ascension, and final judgment were all dispensable. Against traditional ideas of heaven and hell, he suggested that "there will one day be a universal restoration of all souls."[27] In his view, everyone will be saved in the end because God is only love, with no wrath or judgment.

Schleiermacher was in the pulpit once or twice a week for the last forty-five years of his life. We can clearly recognize his theology in one of his sermons, "The Wrath of God," given at Trinity Church in Berlin in 1830. Right at the start of the sermon, he said:

25. Niebuhr, *Kingdom of God in America*, 193.

26. Paulson, "Wrath of God," 245. Paulson is right that "the liberal gospel's approach did not intend merely to be careful when talking about God's wrath, but sought to abolish God's wrath as inappropriate to proper dogma" (246).

27. Originally published in 1821–1822, Schleiermacher revised this work in 1830, just four years prior to his death. Citations here come from Friedrich Schleiermacher, *Christian Faith*, 730, 420.

As the subject of our meditation today, then, I want to suggest this: that we have no cause or directive for setting up this idea of the wrath of God as something grounded in Christianity, as something essential to faith, or even as a proper doctrine. On the contrary, the more we focus our own attention and that of others on this notion, the further we depart from the true spirit of Christianity.[28]

In the heart of the sermon, Schleiermacher claimed that no one could be "helped by any doctrine of the wrath of God." He preached that, "we do not need a doctrine of divine wrath to lead others to Christ." Rather, if we tell people God is holy and wrathful, they may never recover from this distorted introduction to the faith. He believed there was nothing to be gained and much to be lost from teaching God's wrath against sin.[29]

With rhetorical flourish, Schleiermacher concluded his sermon by stating, "now is the time to summon humanity, not to flee God's wrath into the bosom of the Son," since "the true power of Christianity will shine forth ever more brightly the more we lose all false fear of God's wrath, the more we all unlock the only saving knowledge of God: that God is love. Amen."[30] All we need is God's love, and this means no wrath or judgment.

GOD'S LOVE WITHOUT WRATH IN EARLY AMERICAN PROTESTANT LIBERALISM (JEFFERSON)

While Schleiermacher was busy revising the Christian faith in Germany, Thomas Jefferson was doing much the same in America. In the year of his victorious presidential election, 1804, Jefferson systematically separated what he thought were the real teachings of Jesus from the false teachings he believed were also in the Bible. Jefferson snipped the four Gospels into pieces—retaining the material he approved of and simply discarding the rest. Jefferson cut and pasted the old-fashioned way, without a computer, assembling what he believed were the genuine teachings of Jesus in

28. Schleiermacher, "Wrath of God," 152–53.

29. Ibid., 153, 159–61. When Jesus spoke of judgment, Schleiermacher argued that he was merely using this common, traditional idea as a point of departure for his own teaching, while not affirming it himself (*Life of Jesus*, 235, 238). Another strategy of Schleiermacher was to discount Jesus' proclamations of judgment as non-literal (*Life of Jesus*, 332).

30. Schleiermacher, "Wrath of God," 164–65.

double columns on forty-six sheets of paper. Thus he produced what is sometimes dubbed the "Jefferson Bible."[31]

It is not surprising that Matthew 3:7 and Luke 3:7 did not make Jefferson's approved list, because in these verses John the Baptist asked people, "who warned you to flee from the coming wrath?" Jefferson also chose to leave out most of John's Gospel, thus avoiding "embarrassing" passages on God's judgment, such as John 3:36 ("whoever believes in the Son has eternal life, but whoever rejects the Son will not see life, for God's wrath remains on him") and John 12:48 ("there is a judge for the one who rejects me and does not accept my words; that very word which I spoke will condemn him at the last day"). The "Jefferson Bible" ends with Jesus' crucifixion, and includes no account of his resurrection—which apparently was dispensable for Jefferson, as for Schleiermacher.

Fifteen years later Jefferson produced a related work, *The Life and Morals of Jesus*. Here he separated the contents of the Gospels into: (1) "things impossible, of superstitions, fanaticisms, and fabrications," (2) "sublime ideas of the supreme being, aphorisms and precepts of the purest morality and benevolence," and (3) verses "which we may with probability ascribe to Jesus himself."[32] Jefferson's work paralleled that of Schleiermacher in the sense that both of these Protestant liberals felt free to accept some aspects of biblical teaching while rejecting those they found disagreeable. This established pattern of Protestant liberalism was followed a few generations later by another influential German theologian, Albrecht Ritschl.

GOD'S LOVE WITHOUT WRATH IN LATE NINETEENTH-CENTURY LIBERALISM (RITSCHL)

Like Schleiermacher, Ritschl believed that God may be "conceived in general as love." Ritschl said that according to the older theology, God's wrath referred to God's "fixed purpose to punish sin," but in his newer proposal "no validity can be assigned to the idea of the wrath of God." People may experience the false impression that once they were under God's wrath, but are now under God's mercy. However, in view of "the

---

31. Jefferson, *Philosophy of Jesus* and *The Life and Morals of Jesus*.

32. Jefferson, *Life and Morals of Jesus*, 38. According to Adams, Jefferson believed the true and false precepts of Jesus were "as easily distinguishable as diamonds in a dunghill" (28).

antecedent and never-failing love of God," considering oneself as under God's wrath must be rejected as a theological delusion.[33] In Ritschl's view, despite what people may think, in reality everyone is under God's love and never under God's wrath.

Ritschl knew that historically Christ had been viewed as "the propitiation for our sins" or "the Lamb which bears the sins of the world." But in response to "the idea that Christ suffered the punishment for the sins of humanity as punishment," Ritschl declared, "I repudiate this view absolutely." He was adamant that "Christ did not come into contact with God's wrath."[34] Given Ritschl's understanding of God's character (only love and no wrath against sin) and his view of Christ's death (not bearing the punishment for sin), "the very possibility of the Judgment is methodologically excluded" so "nowhere in Ritschl's theology can it be said that the world is under the Judgment of God."[35]

According to Ritschl, people do not need to be saved from God's judgment, but rather they need to be saved from the error of thinking that God is a judge. We need to be rescued not from God's *actual* wrath against sin but from *believing* in God's wrath at all. Like Schleiermacher, Ritschl presumed that in the end everyone would be saved; so he maintained that there was no place for preaching the wrath of God since it holds no prospect for edifying the hearers.[36] Once again, in our theology, all we need is love.

TWENTIETH-CENTURY LIBERAL PROTESTANT REJECTION OF GOD'S WRATH (HANSON)

The same message was carried on in the twentieth-century by theologian Anthony Hanson. He argued that if we believed that God was angry at sin then, "we cannot avoid maintaining that in some sense the Son endured the wrath of the Father," a view which entails "strain and violence to our God-given sense of moral justice." Hanson was repulsed at the idea of Jesus suffering the penalty of God's wrath in the place of sinners. And he

---

33. Ritschl, *Christian Doctrine of Justification and Reconciliation*, 319, 322, 323, 324. This work was originally published as a multi-volume set during the years 1870–1874.

34. Ibid., 565, 569, 572.

35. James Martin, *Last Judgment in Protestant Theology from Orthodoxy to Ritschl*, 200, 206.

36. Ritschl, *Christian Doctrine of Justification and Reconciliation*, 323, 368, 630.

argued that Christians need not believe this doctrine of the atonement, because we do not have to believe the whole Bible, but only its most recent, enlightened parts. In the end, Hanson concluded that, "in the New Testament the wrath is never appeased or propitiated; neither is God or Christ ever described as angry or as being angry."[37]

Of course, Hanson had to face "problem passages" that seemed to contradict his claims, such as Mark 3:5, which speaks of Jesus being angry. Hanson responded that "one cannot argue directly from the fact that our Lord showed certain human emotions to the conclusion that those emotions must be attributable to God the Father." Another problem passage for Hanson is Romans 2:8–9: "But for those who are self-seeking and who reject the truth and follow evil, there will be wrath and anger. There will be trouble and distress for every human being who does evil: first for the Jew, then for the Gentile." Here Hanson used the idea of evolutionary progress within the Bible to argue that Paul's thoughts early in the epistle to the Romans were immature (and therefore may be rejected) in comparison with his thoughts later in the same letter (which should be accepted).[38]

When a passage did not fit his pre-existing theology, Hanson could dismiss it as early and immature, but this strategy did not work with the epistles of Jude and 2 Peter, which are among the latest writings in the New Testament. With no other theological maneuvers at his disposal, Hanson simply rejected these Scriptures outright. He said:

> Jude and 2 Peter together show us the low-water mark of the New Testament conception of judgment. In both we meet a crude and materialistic conception of both judgment and divine punishment, used in a violent and intemperate manner to bludgeon adversaries. The restraint and insight of the rest of the New Testament stand out all the more clearly by contrast. This fact alone should surely prove the non-apostolical origin of these two Epistles.[39]

In Protestant liberalism (whether Schleiermacher, Jefferson, Ritschl, or Hanson) we see a clear pattern. They use human reasoning and experience to decide in advance that God must be only love and no wrath. On this basis they then dismiss "disagreeable" aspects of biblical revelation. Over the years, these thinkers have had a huge impact on liberal seminary

37. Hanson, *Wrath of the Lamb*, 193–4, 9, 179 and 69.

38. Ibid., 114, 88.

39. Ibid., 155, 157–58.

professors, who have trained countless pastors, who in turn have influenced thousands of congregations through their preaching and counseling. The endpoint of this trajectory is illustrated by the recent writings of a famous liberal bishop.

TWENTY-FIRST-CENTURY LIBERAL PROTESTANT
REJECTION OF GOD'S JUDGMENT (SPONG)

John Shelby Spong served in the Episcopalian Church for forty-five years, including twenty-four years as the bishop of Newark, New Jersey. Spong was continually embroiled in controversies of one sort or another. In the 1970s, he started to question whether the Bible really teaches that Jesus is divine. In the 1980s, he called for Christians to revise their traditional sexual views and he began to ordain practicing homosexuals to the priesthood. In the mid-1990s, Spong suggested that Jesus might have been Mary Magdalene's husband and that Jesus' bodily resurrection was not an essential belief.

Then in 1998 Spong wrote a book whose title says it all, *Why Christianity Must Change or Die*. In this work, he explicitly denied that people are sinners, that God is a judge, and that Jesus died to save sinners. Spong boldly declared that, "I would choose to loathe rather than to worship a deity who required the sacrifice of his son." He was equally fearless in saying, "I must dismiss the idea of God as a record-keeping deity before whom I shall appear on the day of judgment to have my eternal destination announced." Still, Spong claimed to be a person of faith, that is, "a believer who lives in the being of God, who loves with the love of God." Spong took the liberal trajectory to its endpoint. In his framework, we do not even need a God who is personal (a real deity that actually exists outside of ourselves); all we need is the power of love.[40]

In a post-retirement book, Spong continued to attack the idea of God as a judge, even a judge who lovingly provides salvation for sinners. In fact, Spong said the whole idea that Jesus suffered the punishment that sinners deserved was "sadomasochism in the heart of Christianity," since it "portrays the holy God involved in a cruel act of divine child abuse that was said to have occurred on a hill called Calvary." To Spong's mind, the idea that "God rescued us from sin by paying the price of our sin through

---

40. Spong, *Why Christianity Must Change or Die*, 95, 210, 219. See also the related statements on page 226.

Jesus" was "grotesque" and "barbaric." He laid his cards plainly on the table with these words:

> Let me state this boldly and succinctly: Jesus did not die for your sins or my sins. That proclamation is theological nonsense. . . . This interpretation of Jesus as the sacrificed victim is a human creation, not a divine revelation. . . . We are not fallen, sinful people who deserve to be punished. We are frightened, insecure people who have achieved the enormous breakthrough into self-consciousness that marks no other creature that has yet emerged from the evolutionary cycle.
>
> The angry deity who judges human life from some heavenly throne might make us feel safe, but this deity always shrinks life, for that is what guilt, fear and righteousness do. That is a god-image that must be broken; but when it is, the traditional way we have told the Jesus story will surely die with it. I believe it *must*. When it does, I think it will be good riddance.[41]

While he certainly qualifies as the most audacious spokesperson for Protestant liberalism, we have seen that Spong stands within a long tradition which desires to embrace God's love while rejecting God's wrath and judgment of sin. Many readers will share my outrage at the presumptuous stances taken by Schleiermacher, Jefferson, Ritschl, Hanson, and Spong. But if we can calm ourselves long enough to step back and see the big picture, we can learn some valuable lessons from the mistakes of Protestant liberalism—which highlights four spiritual landmines that we should avoid.

SPIRITUAL DANGERS ILLUSTRATED BY THE TRADITION OF PROTESTANT LIBERALISM

First, it is dangerous for us to make faulty human reason a higher authority than Scripture in determining what we believe about Jesus. For Protestant liberals, doctrines such as Christ's resurrection, ascension, and future return for judgment were dispensable. By contrast, the apostle Paul said that our salvation rests on the fact that "Christ Jesus, who died—more than that, who was raised to life—is at the right hand of God and is also interceding for us."[42] Paul wrote, "if Christ has not been raised, our preaching

---

41. Spong, *Sins of Scripture*, 169, 171, 172, 173–74 (italics in the original).

42. Romans 8:34. See also 2 Corinthians 5:15 and Hebrews 7:25.

is useless and so is your faith."[43] Put simply, if Paul is right then Protestant liberalism is wrong.

Schleiermacher's view that "there will one day be a universal restoration of all souls" cannot be squared with the teaching of Jesus, who said, "wide is the gate and broad is the road that leads to destruction, and many enter through it. But small is the gate and narrow the road that leads to life, and only a few find it."[44] Without the guidance of Scripture, our reasoning often leads us to faulty theological beliefs.[45]

When Schleiermacher encountered disagreeable sayings of Jesus, he decided they must not be literal or factual. When Jefferson came across such sayings, he took scissors and cut them out from his Bible. When Ritschl ran into biblical passages about people being under God's wrath, he dismissed these beliefs as theological delusions. Hanson advised people to believe only the "enlightened" parts of the Bible (which he identified for them) and to reject the idea that Jesus endured the wrath of the Father on the cross. Spong said the notion that Jesus died for people's sins amounted to barbaric, grotesque divine child abuse that we must eliminate from the faith. In each case these thinkers granted ultimate authority to their reason or experiential intuition about what God must be like, rather than allowing the revelation of Scripture to determine their views.

Of course, the capacity to reason ought to be celebrated as a good gift from God—part of what makes us human. When illuminated by the Holy Spirit, our minds are important vehicles by which we come to know God. Proper reasoning is necessary to rightly understand God's word and God's world. The problem arises when we set fallen human reason as the judge *over* Scripture and give more credence to what we think God must be like than what God has revealed to us in the Bible. The tradition of Protestant liberalism shows us how such an approach can easily end up in theological disaster—as with the blunt denial that Jesus came to save human sinners by dying in our place.

Second, it is dangerous for us to use purely pragmatic standards (what seems to help people) rather than Scripture to govern what we preach and teach. Schleiermacher said there was "no cause for speaking of God's wrath," since no one is "helped by any doctrine of the wrath of God."

---

43. 1 Corinthians 15:14. See also the following verses in 1 Corinthians 15:15–23.

44. Matthew 7:13–4. See also the parallel passage in Luke 13:23–24.

45. See my related arguments in Moroney, *Noetic Effects of Sin.*

Jefferson snipped passages on God's wrath out of his Bible. Ritschl said, "no validity can be assigned to the idea of the wrath of God," and it is purposeless to talk about it. Hanson said we should not teach this doctrine because it is "crude" and strains our sense of moral justice. Spong said the idea of God's wrath shrinks our lives and promotes a distorted image of God. According to the tradition of Protestant liberalism, we have no good reason for believing in God's wrath and no right to teach or preach about God's wrath because it holds no prospect for edifying the hearers.

This liberal approach is completely at odds with the entire canon of Scripture. In the book of Isaiah alone, God's wrathful judgment is likened to a flood, a rod, a storm, consuming warfare, a cup filled with wine, a winepress, and a fire.[46] The New Testament authors also highlighted God's wrath against sin—in all four gospels, Paul's writings, the book of Hebrews, the first epistle of John, and the book of Revelation.[47] There is a crucial difference between God displaying *slow* anger against sin (which the Bible teaches) and God displaying *no* anger against sin (which Protestant liberalism teaches).[48]

As a theologian once said, "the temptation to reduce God to love alone is strong, especially when we fear His wrath or seek to flee from His justice."[49] This temptation, however, must be resisted, and one way to resist it is to allow Scripture to determine what we preach and teach about God. When we adopt this approach, we find that "there are few things stressed more strongly in the Bible than the reality of God's work as Judge."[50] The biblical witness is a more reliable guide to what people really need to hear than our pragmatic sense of what is helpful. Do we really think we know better than God? When we are ashamed to speak of God's wrath, consider what one Bible scholar said:

> [T]he biblical writers are not embarrassed when they treat the theme [of God's wrath]. This is surely because, for them, the wrath of God is an entirely just and therefore admirable display of holi-

46. Isaiah 8:6–8, 10:5–6, 30:30, 42:25, 51:17–23, 63:3–6, and 66:15–16.

47. Matthew 3:7–12; Mark 3:5, 10:14; Luke 3:7–18; John 3:35–36; Romans 1:18, 2:5, 2:8, 4:15, 5:9; Hebrews 3:10—11, 4:3; 1 John 2:2, 4:10; and Revelation 6:15–17, 14:9–20, 15:1–8, 16:1–21.

48. On God's slow anger against sin, see Exodus 34:6–7, Psalm 78:38, Romans 2:4, and 2 Peter 3:15.

49. Sproul, *Character of God*, 151.

50. Packer, *Knowing God*, 138.

ness as it confronts sin. To be embarrassed by what Scripture so clearly and repeatedly sets out as belonging to the character of God when he deals with rebels is not the stance of sophistication and moral superiority. Rather, it is the stance of arrogant disbelief. What right does the creature ever have to be embarrassed by the Creator?[51]

Jesus is never reported as being ashamed of God's wrath or the Old Testament judgment stories. Instead, he spoke of this material freely, in order to warn the people of his day.[52]

Third, another grave danger which the liberal tradition illustrates, and to which we are all susceptible, is that of making God in our own image. In the famous words of one theologian, our sinful nature is "a perpetual factory of idols" that shapes God to our own liking.[53] In its rawest form, we rebelliously try to swap places with God. Instead of us serving God and fitting into the agenda of God's kingdom, we want God to serve us and fit into the agendas of our personal kingdoms. So, we try to eliminate wrath from our concept of God and instead picture God as a deity of all-accepting love who serves us.

The stakes are at a premium for any who follow the path of Protestant liberalism and reject biblical ideas of God's wrath to shape a different image of God. As one theologian said, "if there is no wrath there is no salvation. If God does not take action against sinners, then sinners are in no danger and do not need salvation. Only when we take seriously the wrath of God against sinners do we put real meaning into the salvation that Christ wrought on Calvary."[54] When he considers the mysterious dealings of God with humans, Paul insists that it is not the role of the clay to tell the potter what he must be like. As Paul says in Romans 9:22, "who are you, O man, to talk back to God?"

Fourth, Protestant liberalism demonstrates how dangerous it is for us not to warn people of God's coming judgment. The Bible is full of warnings to help us avoid spiritual landmines. The Psalmist says God's commands are like big, bright warning signs. God commissioned the prophet Ezekiel specifically to warn the Israelites to turn from their wicked ways. In Paul's farewell to the Ephesian elders he reminded them that "for three years I

51. Carson, "Wrath of God," 62–3.

52. Matthew 11:21–4, 24:37–39; Luke 17:26–30, 17:32.

53. Calvin, *Institutes of the Christian Religion*. Book One, chapter 11, section 8 (p. 108).

54. Morris, "Wrath of God," 732.

never stopped warning each of you night and day with tears." The Old Testament prophets and New Testament apostles repeatedly warned of God's coming judgment on wicked people who did not turn from their sins and did not seek forgiveness from God.[55]

When there is a real danger, the most loving thing is to warn people. Loving parents warn their children about touching hot stoves and crossing busy streets. As their spiritual parent, Paul told the Corinthians, "I am not writing this to shame you, but to warn you, as my dear children."[56] When we speak of a God who is only love with no judgment or wrath against sin, as many Protestant liberals do, we lose an essential component of the gospel and actually deprive our hearers of needed warnings that can be expressions of love given out of concern for their well-being.

CONCLUSION

Chapter three documented the widespread tendency today to focus on God's love but neglect God's judgment, even though God's judgment was a foundational teaching and core component of New Testament preaching. Chapter four has traced the history of a few movements (Marcionism and Protestant Liberalism) that promoted belief in a "God of love" who is never wrathful against sin. Collectively, these two chapters have told the story of problems that arise when we believe in a God who loves and never judges.

These chapters also fit into the larger story of this book, namely that we encounter serious problems when we believe in a God who judges but does not love (part one) or when we believe in a God who loves but does not judge (part two). This brings us to a major turning point in the book. So far we have shown that the options of "judgment without love" and "love without judgment" do not stand up to what the Bible teaches about God and they do not work out very well in life. Part three of the book suggests an alternative that sounds simple but has been surprisingly elusive for people to hold onto over the years—that we embrace an image of God which keeps both his love and his judgment together. One-sided views just will not do. So, if you are thirsty for a full-orbed understanding of God that attempts to be faithful to the whole of Scripture, read on.

---

55. Psalm 19; Ezekiel 3 and 33; Acts 20:31.

56. 1 Corinthians 4:14. See also Colossians 1:28 and 1 Thessalonians 5:14.

Questions for Reflection and Discussion

1. Describe a time when you have heard the God of the Old Testament contrasted with the God of the New Testament, maybe in a way that sounded similar to Marcion.

2. Which example of God's love and mercy in the Old Testament struck you the most?

3. What is really lost when we neglect the New Testament teaching on God's wrath?

4. Which of the five Protestant liberals caused the strongest reaction in you, and why?

5. Do any of the spiritual dangers listed at the end apply to you personally? Explain.

PART THREE

Love and Judgment Together

5

Staying out of the Ditches

Contemporary Models of God's Love and Wrath

WHEN I WAS A boy, one of my favorite places in the world was my grandparents' cabin in the woods. Many a weekend, especially in the summertime, our family would pile into the station wagon (decked out with a travel carrier on top and fake wood paneling on the sides), and we would head for the cabin. In those days there was a lot less concern with seatbelts, so I often spent most of the hour-long drive playing freely in the back of the car with my brothers and sister. Once we reached the property gate, we could hardly contain our excitement. But we also knew that in the dark it could be tricky for Dad to navigate the narrow, winding driveway from the gate to the cabin. If he was not careful, we could easily slide off into the deep ditch on the side of the skinny dirt road.

So far this book has focused on the ditches. Steer a little too far to the right and a person or a whole church can get stuck in the ditch of "judgment without love." Go too far to the left and we can end up in the other ditch of "love without judgment." It is easy to fall into these errors, as we have seen in the annals of church history and in our images of God today. That leads us to the crucial question for this book: how do we stay on the "road of truth" that avoids the perilous ditches which lurk so dangerously on either side?

After four chapters highlighting the ditches to avoid, we are more than ready to consider options that do not isolate God's attributes of love and judgment from one another, but instead attempt to join them together. But before we try to understand how God's love relates to his judgment, we need to be reminded why these two attributes are so important and why we should cherish them both. Then we will explore several recent efforts to relate God's love to a key manifestation of God's judgment—his wrath.

CHERISHING GOD'S LOVE

Most of us naturally cherish God's love. It is easy to echo Charles Wesley's hymn from the eighteenth century: "Amazing love! How can it be that thou, my God, shouldst die for me?" Christians happily join in singing the nineteenth-century hymn that extols "the deep, deep love of Jesus—vast, unmeasured, boundless, free; rolling as a mighty ocean in its fullness over me." Many still resonate with the early twentieth-century hymn that testifies, "when nothing else could help, love lifted me." Composers in the twenty-first-century continue to write contemporary songs that prompt us to celebrate God's incredible love.

One present-day pastor wrote an entire book on God's love and concluded with these inspiring words: "Ultimately the love of God is the basis for all our hopes. It is the object of our deepest longings. It is the source and fulfillment of our faith.... His love absolutely permeates and envelops every aspect of our lives in Christ.... In light of the glories of divine love, how can we not be utterly lost in wonder, love, and praise?"[1]

To appreciate God's love, all we have to do is consider what the world would be like without it. Imagine if God were neutral toward us—not unloving but simply lacking love for people. Suppose God related to humans in the same way that most of us relate to beetles. We are aware of their existence and understand their place in the ecosystem, but we are really not all that interested in them or concerned about them. Even entomologists who know a lot about beetles do not set their deep affections on them. Imagine if God knew all about us but did not bother much with us, and never used his power for our good. Such a God would not seek out relationships with humans. Perhaps such a God would not even take the trouble to create us in the first place. Certainly a God who did not love his people would not find delight in blessing them, as the Bible says he does.[2]

---

1. MacArthur, Jr. *Love of God*, 168–69.

2. On God delighting in his people, see Deuteronomy 30:9; 2 Samuel 22:20; 1 Kings 10:9; 2 Chronicles 9:8; Psalm 18:19, 147:11, 149:4; Proverb 11:20, 12:22; Isaiah 62:4, 65:18–19; Jeremiah 31:20; Zephaniah 3:17.

Even more frightening, imagine if God were all-knowing and all-powerful but rather than being a God of love, God was malicious instead. Such a God would know exactly how to torment us, would have the power to carry out his cruel plans, and would enjoy inflicting agony upon us. That's a scary thought! Paul comforted the Christians in Rome (and, by extension, all believers today) when he asked, "if God is for us, who can be against us?"[3] If God were malicious rather than loving, everyone would face the horrifying question, "if God is against us, who can be for us?" We would be in a totally hopeless situation! It is no trite statement, but a profound truth, when we say "Thank God for his love." So, with just a little reflection on what life might otherwise be like, God's people gratefully cherish his love.

CHERISHING GOD'S JUDGMENT

Cherishing God's judgment, by contrast, does not come easily to most of us, perhaps because we instinctively recoil when we think about God's perfect holiness and justice exposing our sin. But the authors of Scripture cherished God's judgment. The Psalmist saw God's righteous, truthful judgments as cause for *rejoicing, gladness, and jubilation* (Psalm 96:10–13). Zion *rejoiced* and the villages of Judah were *glad* because of the Lord's judgments (97:8). The book of Psalms exhorts us to respond to the Lord's righteous judgment with *clapping and singing* (98:8–9). When is the last time your Sunday morning church service began with a call to worship that focused on God's judgments?

When God judges the earth and sweeps the wicked away, the Psalmist proclaims, "the righteous will be *glad* when they are avenged" (58:10). The likely picture in the Psalmist's mind is "a civil case with himself as the plaintiff," so that as he brings his case into God's courtroom, he "hopes for a resounding triumph with heavy damages."[4] The Psalmist looks forward to seeing God right every wrong. The Psalmist said that the Lord's *wrath* against people actually brings the Lord *praise* (76:10). Imagine your church worship leader starting things off with a song that praised God for his wrath!

Of course, some have said that such a perspective is limited to the Old Testament (remember Marcion), but the fact is that God is praised

3. Romans 8:31.
4. Lewis, *Reflections on the Psalms*, 10.

for his wrathful judgments in the New Testament, too. The saints, apostles, and prophets in heaven are called to rejoice over the great city of Babylon because God has judged her for the way she treated them (Revelation 18:20). Then John reports (in Revelation 19:1–3) hearing what sounds like the roar of a great multitude in heaven shouting:

> "Hallelujah! Salvation and glory and power belong to our God, for true and just are his judgments. He has condemned the great prostitute who corrupted the earth by her adulteries. He has avenged on her the blood of his servants." And again they shouted: "Hallelujah! The smoke from her goes up for ever and ever."

As shocking as it is to our ears, heaven's "Hallelujah Chorus" in Revelation 19 focuses on God's judgments. The word "Hallelujah" (or "Alleluia") means "Praise the Lord." The only time this word appears in the entire New Testament is in Revelation chapter 19, when a great heavenly multitude praises God for avenging the blood of his servants and condemning those who adulterously corrupted the earth. In the end, God will be praised not merely for his love but also because "true and just are his judgments."

As with God's love, our appreciation for God's judgment grows as we consider what the world would be like without it. In such a world, those who massacred people of other ethnicities would *never* be called to account by God for the evils of their genocide. The Lord would *never* judge serial child rapists who successfully avoided earthly arrest. The scales of justice would remain *permanently* out of balance. In the end God would *not* right every wrong. The Lord's statement, "vengeance is mine, I will repay" would actually be *false*.[5] When we think hard about what this universe would be like without it, we can see that *God's judgment is a good thing to be cherished.* As one theologian said:

> The truth is that part of God's moral perfection is his perfection in judgment. Would a God who did not care about the difference between right and wrong be a good and admirable Being? Would a God who put no distinction between the beasts of history, the Hitlers and Stalins (if we dare use names), and his own saints, be morally praiseworthy and perfect? Moral indifference would be an imperfection in God, not a perfection. But not to judge the world would be to show moral indifference. The final proof that God is

5. Deuteronomy 32:35, Romans 12:17, Hebrews 10:30.

a perfect moral Being, not indifferent to questions of right and wrong, is that he has committed himself to judge the world.[6]

So, God's judgment is a good thing! But exactly how does it relate to his love? That is a difficult and controversial question. When I first taught this material in an adult education class, one woman said, "I've been a Christian for thirty years and have always tried to bring God's love and judgment together because I know they are both true, but I don't know how to do it." The remainder of this chapter explores five possible models for relating God's love to one of the key expressions of his judgment—namely, God's wrath against sin. In the end, I will argue that the last model is the most promising one.

MODEL #1: INTERNAL CONFLICT WITHIN GOD BETWEEN HIS LOVE AND WRATH

A young boy grows up with a strong sense of right and wrong. He thinks that when people break the rules they should face the consequences. He enters the police academy, and spends his first few years on the job directing the drug awareness program, mainly giving educational talks in the middle schools. Eventually he becomes the chief of police for his metro area. Then one Saturday morning when he needs a set of jumper cables, he rummages through the trunk of his teen son's car and finds a stash of cocaine. His mind swirls as he storms into his son's room and confronts him with the evidence. At first the teen says he has never seen the stuff before. Then he says that last night at a party he let some friends use the car, so it must be theirs. But after Dad rifles through the chest of drawers and finds more evidence, the son comes clean about his illegal drug use.

The father is torn up inside. He is so angry at his son he could strangle him, but when the father gets a little distance from the explosive situation, he also wants to talk heart to heart with his boy and give him a hug. The chief of police knows that according to the law he could have his son sent to the county detention center for minors, but in this relationship he is a parent first and a cop second. In the end, he flushes the drugs and tries to set things right at home without any arrest or legal action. Fatherly love wins out.

Perhaps it is like that with God. In the aftermath of World War II, Kazoh Kitamori, a Japanese theologian, wrote a famous book that

6. Packer, *Knowing God*, 143.

focused on "the pain of God." He wanted to avoid the mistake of liberal theology, which embraced God's love and rejected his wrath. His solution was to propose "the pain of God as a synthesis of his wrath and love."[7] But Kitamori's synthesis was an uneasy one because he saw the two elements of love and wrath in a state of conflict with each other. He put it this way:

> The "pain" of God reflects his will to love the object of his wrath. ... God who must sentence sinners to death fought with God who wishes to love them. The fact that this fighting God is not two different gods but the same God causes his pain. Here heart is opposed to heart within God.[8]

What was the outcome of the "heart opposed to heart" and "fighting within God"? Kitamori said that "the pain of God means that the love of God had conquered the wrath of God in the midst of the *historical* world deserving his wrath" and that "the pain of God is his love conquering the inflexible wrath of God."[9] According to this model, there was an internal conflict within God because of the two warring principles of wrath and love, but thankfully God's love conquered his wrath—much as it did with the chief of police.

What can we say about this model? Positively, it was an improvement on what Marcion and Protestant liberals said earlier, in dismissing God's wrath altogether (see chapter four). Kitamori's model rightly affirmed that God's wrath is real, and it grappled seriously with how God's wrath relates to his love. His model also advanced beyond the liberal teaching of universalism (that ultimately all people will be saved) by stating that "unbelievers can never be united to God as long as they are in their natural condition."[10] Kitamori realized that due to God's holiness, unbelieving sinners are under God's wrath.

The major shortcoming in Kitamori's model, however, is the way it sets God's wrath and love in opposition to each other, suggesting that

---

7. Kitamori, *Theology of the Pain of God*, 26. Related comments are found on pages 16 and 24.

8. Ibid., 21.

9. Ibid., 34–35 (italics in the original). See also page 37.

10. Ibid., 62. This accords with John 3:36 and other Scriptural passages.

there is internal conflict within God.[11] But there is no warfare going on within God. God is never at cross-purposes with himself, with one "part" of God fighting against another "part." In the words of one theologian, "God's nature is not characterized by inner tension. Whereas some have pictured him as torn by conflict between his love and his justice, this is not the way he is. His love is a just love, and his justice is a loving justice."[12] We must never separate God's attributes and pit them *against* one another because they are all ultimately united. So, we need to find another way to understand God's love and wrath.

MODEL #2: GOD'S WRATH AS SUBORDINATE TO GOD'S LOVE

A wife loves her husband and truly wants what is best for him. She is the best mate imaginable, lavishing affection and gifts on her spouse. Yet, for some mysterious reason, her husband does not reciprocate her love and even cheats on her every so often. She desires a close relationship without conflict, but sometimes she is so wounded by her husband that she finds herself yelling at him, though she really does not like to do that. She tells her husband it is her deep love that causes her occasional outbursts of anger.

Can that story help us understand God? Contemporary theologians Clark Pinnock and Robert Brow recognized problems with suggesting, as Kitamori had, that "God had competing and even conflicting attributes." In their view, "if God were wrath in the same way that he is love, God would be internally schizophrenic." So, in 1994 they suggested an alternative model in which "God's wrath is in the service of his love. Love and wrath are not equally ultimate in the divine nature like two parallel attributes: instead, wrath is subordinate to love." Within their model, "wrath arises in relation to sinners who spurn divine love. Betrayal calls for a

---

11. Kitamori even argues that "the pain of God is his 'essence'" (ibid., 47, 81). Though Kitamori occasionally speaks of God's pain as "uniting" God's wrath and love (58–59, 127), his basic framework presents God's wrath and love as opposites that fight or conflict with each other, such that God's wrath must be "conquered" or "overcome" (34, 35, 37, 83, 109, 111, 112). Kitamori explicitly states that God's wrath "is the reality in conflict with his love" (108) such that "wrath and love cannot be compatible; wrath must be overcome by love" (112).

12. Erickson, *God the Father Almighty*, 291.

vigorous response; God's wrath arises from injured love.... Paradoxically, if God is angry with us it is because he loves us."[13]

This model proposes that God would prefer never to be angry, but sometimes God becomes angry because he loves us so much. Pinnock and Brow put it this way:

> God does not like anger in us because he does not even like it in himself. Think of the book of Jonah, which tells how God wants to repent of the evil that he said he would do to Nineveh. He really longs for the Ninevites to repent so that he will not have to judge them. God does not want to be angry, and his wrath only happens when people remain stubbornly impenitent, when they leave God no alternative but to act in judgment. But even then God would much rather do them good, because he is compassionate by nature.... Because God's anger is rooted in his love for us, it is actually distasteful to him. It is a tragic necessity, not something God ever delights in. It causes him suffering and means he must suspend his mercy for a time.[14]

How should we assess this model? On the positive side, it picks up on biblical portrayals of how people spurn God's love.[15] This model also draws attention to the fact that God's love is not always treated in parallel fashion with God's wrath. The Old Testament describes the LORD as "the compassionate and gracious God, *slow to anger, abounding in love* and faithfulness, maintaining love to thousands, and forgiving wickedness, rebellion and sin."[16] Slow to anger and abounding in love is far different than slow to love and abounding in anger. The New Testament never says "God is wrath" in the same way it says "God is love." Love has always existed eternally within the very being of God, but before there was any sin in the world there was no expression of God's wrath. So, it is true that God's wrath does not parallel God's love exactly.

But this model also has significant problems. To speak of people as "leaving God no alternative" suggests that in some sense humans call the

---

13. Pinnock and Brow, *Unbounded Love*. Quotes in this paragraph are from pages 67–68. The idea that God's wrath is injured love also appears in Moltmann, *Crucified God*, 272.

14. Pinnock and Brow, *Unbounded Love*, 69.

15. For echoes of people spurning God's love, see the book of Hosea, Isaiah 1:4, and Matthew 23:37.

16. See, among other many other passages, Exodus 34:6–7a, Numbers 14:18, Psalm 86:15, and Joel 2:13.

shots and God is a reluctant responder who is forced back into a corner. This picture of God as hemmed in by "tragic necessity" does not fit the biblical portrayal of God's sovereignty, according to which God "works out everything in conformity with the purpose of his will."[17]

Another problem with this model is the notion that God's anger is "distasteful to him." For instance, the Old Testament gives us no hint that God wished he could forgive Uzzah, but was forced to kill him, even though it was unpleasant. The narratives simply describe how "Uzzah reached out and took hold of the ark of God," and "the Lord's anger burned against Uzzah because of his irreverent act; therefore God struck him down and he died there beside the ark of God." Or to take a New Testament example, when people proclaimed Herod to be divine, we read that "immediately, because Herod did not give praise to God, an angel of the Lord struck him down, and he was eaten by worms and died." There is no indication that God's wrath was distasteful to him. The same is true of many other outpourings of God's wrath, as depicted in the book of Revelation.[18]

Lastly, this model speaks of God suspending his mercy in order to vent his wrath. Like the first model, this one seems to place God's mercy and wrath in opposition to each other in such a way that they cannot both be present at the same time. But the Hebrew prophet Habakkuk apparently saw things differently when he called out to God, "in wrath remember mercy" (3:2). Habakkuk believed that the Lord could show mercy right in the midst of wrathful punishment on Judah. So, it appears that God's attributes of wrath and mercy can co-exist, as will be explained later in more detail in the fifth model. But before getting there, we will look at two other models suggested by contemporary theologians.

MODEL #3: GOD'S WRATH AS AN EXPRESSION OF GOD'S LOVE

Loving parents want what is best for their children. So, they often intervene when their kids begin to hang around with the wrong crowd, engage in destructive behaviors, and grow more distant at home. Mom and Dad may even take actions that cost them something personally because they

---

17. Ephesians 1:11. See also Psalm 115:3.

18. 1 Samuel 6:6–7/1 Chronicles 13:9–10; Acts 12:22–23; Revelation 11:18, 14:9–10, 14:19–20, 16:1, 16:19.

are willing to sacrifice for their children's long-term interests. Can these reflections on parenting help us to understand something about God?

In 2003, theologian Baxter Kruger published a book which criticized the view that "the loving side of the Father sends the Son to suffer the punishment demanded by the holy side of the Father" in order that "the hands of the Father's love can at last be untied and He is free to embrace us." Kruger proposed an alternative model which views God's wrath as an expression of God's love. According to Kruger, "God is for us and therefore opposed—utterly, eternally and passionately opposed—to our destruction. That opposition, that fiery and passionate and determined 'No!' to the disaster of the Fall, is the proper understanding of the wrath of God. Wrath is not the opposite of love. Wrath is the love of God in action, in opposing action." Or again, Kruger said, "this love of God in action, this agonizing incarnation suffering to convert humanity, is the wrath of God, the fiery and complete opposition of God's love to our destruction." For Kruger, wrath is the triune God's loving plan to undo the Fall and adopt humanity as his own.[19]

In a recent popularization of Kruger's model, the author suggested, by way of provocative questions, that God's wrath is really an expression of God's love: "What if God's wrath is not a caveat, qualification, or even a counterpoint to his love, but an expression of it? What if God grieves sin less because it offends his sensibilities, and more because he hates the way it distorts our perceptions and separates us from him?"[20]

Does this third model "keep us out of the ditches"? Positively, Kruger is right that we should not think of God as divided, in such a way that the Father's "loving side" sends the Son to suffer the punishment required by the Father's "holy side." As the final model will suggest later in the chapter, God is never at cross-purposes with himself and none of God's attributes ultimately conflict with each other. Kruger is also right that Jesus did not "untie God's hands" so that God could love us. Rather than *allowing* God to love us, Jesus shows us *that* God loves sinners, according to the Bible.[21]

---

19. Kruger, *Jesus and the Undoing of Adam*. Quotes in this paragraph are from pages 28, 46–47, and 68–69. The idea that God's wrath is simply an expression of God's love is also found in other theologians, including Lester, *Angry Christian*.

20. Arends, "Grace of Wrath," 64. I cite Arends here because many readers would find Kruger's own explanation of how God's wrath expresses God's love more difficult to follow. For those who are interested, see *Jesus and the Undoing of Adam*, 35, 62, 70.

21. John 3:16; Romans 5:8; 1 John 4:10.

So, Kruger helpfully draws our attention to some popular misunderstandings of what God is like.

The model that Kruger suggests as a corrective to these problems, however, has serious problems of its own. First, while the Bible does not teach that God has two sides (a "holy side" and a "loving side"), it *does* teach that God is holy—that is, morally pure and separate from all that is evil or unclean.[22] And, although Kruger considers it to be the great theological disaster of Western Christianity, the Bible *does* teach that Christ's atoning death makes believers holy through his righteousness imputed to us by faith.[23]

Second, the Bible *does* teach that Christ came to save us from God's wrath—that is, God's firm and settled opposition to sin. Paul tells the Roman Christians, "since we have now been justified by his [Jesus'] blood, how much more shall we be saved from God's wrath through him." A crucial component of redemption is salvation from God's wrath, which cannot possibly denote "the love of God in action," as Kruger contends. Who needs to be saved *from* God's love in action? Though Kruger flatly denies it, Scripture teaches that sinners need to be saved *from* God's holy wrath against sin. God's wrath is especially directed toward the sins of unbelief and disobedience. The antidote is to trust in Christ and obey the one who came to rescue his followers from God's wrath.

New Testament scholars have established that the Greek word often translated as "wrath" (*ŏrgē*) may mean a "state of relatively strong displeasure, with focus on the emotional aspect" or, usually, a "strong indignation

22. Leviticus 10:1–3, 11:44–5; Psalm 5:4–5, 99:1–5; Isaiah 40:25, 57:15; James 1:13; 1 John 1:5.

23. Romans 4:1–5, 1 Corinthians 1:30, 2 Corinthians 5:21. Kruger argues that this sort of "legal language" is the great theological disaster of Western Christianity that has eclipsed the true gospel (*Jesus and the Undoing of Adam*, 41–53). Along with most New Testament scholars, I see such legal language undeniably embedded in Paul's interpretation of the Christ event, which the Christian Church recognizes in its canon. According to the book of Hebrews, the good news is that Jesus' followers "have been made holy through the sacrifice of the body of Jesus Christ once for all," because "Jesus also suffered outside the city gate to make the people holy through his own blood " (Hebrews 10:10, 13:12; see also Hebrews 2:10–11, 10:14).

directed at wrongdoing, with focus on retribution."[24] These definitions make sense of how the word "wrath" is used in the New Testament, but Kruger's proposal of "love of God in action" does not. John the Baptist said to the Pharisees and Sadducees, "You brood of vipers! Who warned you to flee from the coming wrath?" Why warn people to *flee* from the coming "love of God in action"? The Gospel of John says, "whoever rejects the Son will not see life, for God's wrath remains on him." Why would anyone have to worry about rejecting the Son and not seeing life because "God's love in action" remains on him?[25]

Kruger's model suggests that God's wrath is merely an expression of his love—an alluring prospect for those who picture God as only love with no wrath (recall chapters three and four). But love is not God's only attribute. The apostle John who wrote "God is love" also wrote "God is light" in whom there is no darkness.[26] Love is a *true* description of God's character that we should cherish deeply, but it is not a *complete* description of God's character. God is also holy, just, truthful, wise, faithful, etc. God's wrath cannot be reduced simply to a way that God expresses his love. The next model, which allows God's love and wrath each to stand on their own with full integrity, has better prospects.

MODEL #4: BALANCE WITHIN GOD BETWEEN HIS LOVE AND WRATH

In the 1984 hit movie, "The Karate Kid," the concept of balance is a central theme. Mr. Miyagi tells his young protégé Daniel, "Better learn balance. Balance is key. Balance good, karate good. Everything good." A bit later Mr. Miyagi proclaims, "Lesson not just karate only. Lesson for whole life. Whole life have a balance."

---

24. Danker (ed.), *A Greek-English Lexicon*, 720–21. The word *ŏrgē* is used in Matthew 3:7; Mark 3:5; Luke 3:7, 21:23; John 3:36; Romans 1:18, 2:5, 2:8, 3:5, 4:15, 5:9, 9:22, 12:19, 13:4; Ephesians 2:3, 4:31, 5:6; Colossians 3:6, 3:8; 1 Thessalonians 1:10, 2:16, 5:9; 1 Timothy 2:8; Hebrews 3:11, 4:3; James 1:19; and Revelation 6:16, 6:17, 11:18, 14:10, 16:19, 19:15. The related Greek word *thumŏs*, sometimes translated as "anger," can mean "a state of intense displeasure, anger, wrath, rage, indignation" (Danker, *A Greek-English Lexicon*, 461). For a careful study of a dozen Greek words related to the idea of anger, see Chambers, "A Biblical Theology of Godly Human Anger," 116–30.

25. Matthew 3:7 and Luke 3:7; John 3:36.

26. 1 John 1:5, 4:8, 4:16.

There is no doubt that balance is an appealing concept. We usually admire balanced diets, balanced lives, and balanced viewpoints—not to mention balanced checkbooks! Few people like to be described as imbalanced. Whether it is a six-year-old learning to ride her bike, a twenty-six-year-old daredevil crossing a tightrope over Niagara Falls, a forty-six-year-old trying to juggle career and home, or a sixty-six-year-old seeking to enjoy retirement while still serving in the church, each wants to maintain balance.

The concept of balance similarly has been trumpeted as a solution to the puzzle of how God's love relates to his wrath. According to a book published by pastor John MacArthur, Jr. in 1996, the problem with Protestant liberalism was that it upheld "a warped and imbalanced concept of God" and even today "millions are kept in spiritual darkness by a notion of God that is completely out of balance." The antidote to this problem is for us to "maintain a carefully balanced perspective" by realizing that "God's love cannot be isolated from His wrath and vice versa." According to MacArthur, "divine love not only keeps divine wrath in check while God appeals to the sinner—but it also proves that God is just when He finally condemns." MacArthur stressed again and again our need for "balance between God's love and His wrath."[27]

This model avoids many of the problems that beset the three others we have looked at so far. One of MacArthur's arguments for balance comes from his detailed analysis of the first seven verses of the Old Testament book of Nahum. Here we read that "the LORD is a jealous and avenging God; the LORD takes vengeance and is filled with wrath. The LORD takes vengeance on his foes and maintains his wrath against his enemies" (1:2–3). But we also read that "the LORD is good, a refuge in times of trouble. He cares for those who trust him" (1:7). MacArthur observed that "the same God who threatens judgment against the wicked lovingly, compassionately invites sinful souls in despair to find their refuge in Him." MacArthur is right that "Nahum places his accolade to the goodness and mercy of God in the midst of a passage about God's wrath."[28] Since God is revealed in Scripture as one who is *both* loving *and* wrathful, MacArthur properly affirms *both* God's love *and* God's wrath, without diminishing

27. Quotes in this paragraph are from MacArthur, *Love of God*, 9, 41, 18, 30, and 38 (see also 29).

28. Quotes in this paragraph are from ibid., 69, 71.

the full force of either. His model is right to promote this sort of "balance" between God's love and wrath.

On the other hand, it is also possible for us to be misled in our understanding of God if we conceive of "balance" in the wrong way. For many of us, the idea of balance conjures up mental images such as hanging scales in an old-fashioned marketplace, a teeter-totter on a playground, or a tightrope walker at the circus. In each of these instances, the key to maintaining balance is to put equal weight on both sides. When one side offsets the other, then balance is achieved. This sort of mental picture may have prompted MacArthur to speak of "divine love keeping divine wrath in check" or of God's wrath being "tempered by His great patience and lovingkindness."[29]

The problem is that this explanation retains a lingering hint of opposition between God's love and wrath. It sounds as though there are two opposing forces within God, such that God's love restrains his wrath from breaking out. In this formulation, the two attributes seem to work against each other—one keeping the other in check or tempering the other. The final model suggests that it is best to avoid all such oppositional imagery of "rival attributes" and instead view God's love and wrath both as manifestations of his united nature in such a way that none of his attributes really "balance one another out."[30]

MODEL #5: LOVE AND WRATH AS EXPRESSIONS OF GOD'S MULTIFACETED, UNITED CHARACTER

I have a vivid memory of the evening Sue and I were engaged. I arrived at her apartment dressed in a tuxedo with roses in hand. We enjoyed a great dinner, during which I proposed and she accepted. Whew! My cheeks literally hurt from smiling so much. We capped off the night by going to look at a ring I had tentatively picked out. Given Sue's tastes and our budget, I had selected a simple but elegant diamond solitaire. It still looks great on her a quarter century later, and it symbolizes our covenant of love.

---

29. Ibid., 30, 64.

30. Another possible problem with "balance" imagery is that a person might be "balanced" with a 1% appreciation of God's love and a 1% appreciation of God's wrath, while still 99% lacking on both. Another person might be "imbalanced" with a 4% appreciation of God's love and a 2% appreciation of God's wrath. In this case, the "imbalanced" person would actually be further along in their understanding of God than the "balanced" person. Balance, by itself, is not enough—as MacArthur himself would surely agree.

The last model likens God's character to a beautiful, sparkling diamond that can be admired from different angles. Just as each facet of a diamond captures light and reflects it back brilliantly to the human eye, so each of God's attributes reflects a facet of the complete beauty of his character. In the words of one theologian, "each attribute is simply a way of describing one aspect of God's total character or being."[31] This last model denies that God's wrath *conflicts with* his love, that God's wrath is *subordinate to* his love, that God's wrath is merely an *expression of* his love, or that God's wrath and love must be *balanced* against one another. Rather, this last model—assembled from the insights of several theologians— envisions God's wrath and love both as *expressions of God's very nature*. That is, God's wrath and God's love both flow out of *who God is*.[32]

God's Wrath and God's Character

First, as one who is absolutely *holy*, by nature God is firmly and permanently opposed to sin.[33] This helps us understand Psalm 5:4–6: "You are not a God who takes pleasure in evil; with you the wicked cannot dwell. The arrogant cannot stand in your presence; you hate all who do wrong. You destroy those who tell lies; bloodthirsty and deceitful men the Lord abhors." Because God is perfectly holy, God naturally (out of his very nature) opposes evil, wickedness, arrogance, wrongdoing, and dishonesty. Thus, God's wrath may be thought of as "the holiness of God stirred into activity against sin."[34]

Second, as one who *jealously* desires our complete, undivided loyalty, God refuses to share "his bride" with other gods and naturally opposes spiritual adultery in his people.[35] This is the logic behind the command of Deuteronomy 6:14–15: "Do not follow other gods, the gods of the peoples around you; for the LORD your God, who is among you, is a jealous God and his anger will burn against you, and he will destroy you from the

31. Grudem, *Systematic Theology*, 179–80.

32. Though his dominant metaphor is "balance," MacArthur also hints at this final model when he says, of God, that "both love and wrath are reflections of His nature" (*Love of God*, 87).

33. Leviticus 10:1–3, 11:44–45; 1 John 1:5, 3:3–9.

34. Pink, *Attributes of God*, 107.

35. Exodus 20:4–5, 34:13–17; Deuteronomy 4:24. Zephaniah 1:18 connects God's wrath and jealousy. "On the day of the LORD's wrath," we are told, "in the fire of his jealousy the whole world will be consumed."

face of the land." Because God is jealous and rightfully calls for people's exclusive devotion, God's very nature opposes every instance of spiritual unfaithfulness.

Third, as one who is totally *righteous* and whose judicial actions set the standard for what is right, God naturally condemns all unrighteousness and wickedness.[36] Seen in this light, Psalm 7:11 makes good sense: "God is a righteous judge, a God who expresses his wrath every day." Because God is absolutely righteous and just, when he encounters unrighteousness and injustice, wrath is the natural result. And that is a good thing, as we noted at the beginning of the chapter. To sum up what I have said about the last model so far, God is naturally wrathful against sin because of his holy, jealous, righteous character.

God's Love and God's Character

Thankfully, for us sinners, that is not the whole story. As stated earlier, God's character is multifaceted—like a radiant diamond that dazzles us with its many brilliant facets. So, while we stand in awe at God's wrath against sin, we also marvel at his love for sinners. Love and mercy flow freely out of God's compassionate, gracious nature.[37]

The Psalmist knew the LORD to be "a compassionate and gracious God, slow to anger and abounding in love and faithfulness" (86:15), and on that basis he called on the LORD to "turn to me and have mercy on me" (86:16). After his sinful adultery with Bathsheba, David cried out: "Have mercy on me, O God, according to your unfailing love; according to your great compassion blot out my transgressions" (51:1). Since God is merciful and loving in his very nature, we can ask God to show mercy and love to us!

To put it simply, God does what God does because of who God is. Notice the clear link in 1 John 4:8–9 between God's nature (God *is* love) and the actions that flow out of that nature (so God *shows* his love among his people): "Whoever does not love does not know God, because God is love. This is how God showed his love among us: He sent his one and only Son into the world that we might live through him."

36. Psalm 11:5, 19:8–9, 45:7, 119:137–38.

37. Raabe, "The Two 'Faces' of Yahweh: Divine Wrath and Mercy in the Old Testament," 296.

God's very nature is love, with love flowing freely between the Persons of the Trinity.[38] Because God exists as a community of love, it is natural for God to express his love toward people—which is exactly what he does. The Father displays his loving nature by sending his Son into this world to rescue sinners, and the Son displays his loving nature by giving his life as a substitute for others so that they might be saved.[39] The Spirit displays his loving nature by constantly pouring love into believers' hearts.[40] So, as we combine the two components of the last model we have examined so far, we can say that wrath and love are both expressions of God's very nature.

The Unity of God's Character

This last model also maintains that God's nature is united, so that his wrath and love "should never be set in opposition to one another, for they are just different ways of looking at the totality of God's character."[41] That explains why many theologians in the early Church "would never allow themselves to discuss the judgment and wrath of God in isolation from God's goodness and love, since they were at pains to show that these apparent opposites were in fact united in the one true God."[42] This point is vital for us today. We must realize that there is no final contradiction in saying that the God of wrath *is* also the God of love. According to this last model, the best way for us to understand God is to hold all of his attributes together. One Bible scholar put it this way:

> Because God is holy, He must respond with wrath and judgment on sin and disobedience. His righteousness demands that He not leave wickedness unpunished. Such lenience would be contrary to His holy character. But God does not hasten to punish the sinner. Instead, He exercises His attribute of longsuffering. God's prolonged and patient dealings with the wicked should not be interpreted to mean that sin is not serious or does not matter. Rather, God's patience gives the wicked time and opportunity to repent.[43]

38. 1 John 4:8, 4:16; John 3:35, 5:20, 14:31.
39. John 3:16, 10:11, 15:13; Romans 5:8.
40. Romans 5:5, 15:30; Colossians 1:8.
41. Grudem, *Systematic Theology*, 180.
42. Zachman, "Unity of Judgment and Love," 150.
43. Laney, "God's Self-Revelation in Exodus 34:6–8," 46.

Since God's character is both multifaceted and united, our final model suggests that "everything he says or does is fully consistent with all his attributes."[44] For example, consider God's love. Because God is eternal (without beginning or end), his love is an everlasting love.[45] Because God is immutable (unchanging in character, nature, and purposes), his love is an unchanging love—from which Christ's followers can never be separated.[46] Because God is holy (perfectly pure morally), his love is a holy love, and God lovingly disciplines his children so that we might share in his holy nature.[47]

Alternatively, consider God's judgment. Because God is omniscient (knows all things), his judgment is an omniscient judgment.[48] Unlike our judgments, God's judgments are based on complete, accurate knowledge. Because God is perfectly righteous, all of his ways are just, including his judgments.[49] Unlike corrupt human judges, God never judges unjustly. Because God is totally truthful, his judgments are always true judgments.[50] That is why the Psalmist and the multitude in heaven can say, "his judgments are true and righteous."[51] Because God is incredibly patient, he withholds judgment and persistently offers salvation to people for extended periods of time.[52] When we are wronged we often want judgment right away, but God's judgment is a patient judgment that will come in his time, not ours. God's wrathful judgment, as one theologian said, is not

---

44. Grudem, *Systematic Theology*, 180. MacArthur hints at this idea when he says that "love pervades and influences all His attributes" (*The Love of God*, 29).

45. On God's eternal nature, see Psalm 90:2, 1 Timothy 1:17, 2 Peter 3:8, Revelation 1:8. On God's everlasting love, see Jeremiah 31:3 and Ephesians 1:4–5.

46. On God's unchanging nature, see Psalm 102:25–27, Malachi 3:6, Hebrews 6:17–18, James 1:17. On the impossibility of Christ's followers being separated from God's love, see Romans 8:35–39.

47. On God's holy nature, see Leviticus 10:1–3, 11:44–45; Psalm 5:4–6; James 1:13; 1 John 1:5. On God's loving discipline and sharing in his holy nature, see Hebrews 12:5–11, Matthew 5:48, and 2 Peter 1:4. The subject of God's discipline and human discipline is treated at greater length in chapter six.

48. Psalm 147:5, Proverbs 15:3, Matthew 10:29–30, Hebrews 4:13, 1 John 3:20.

49. Deuteronomy 32:4; Psalm 72:1–2, 89:14, 97:2; Jeremiah 9:24; Romans 3:25–26.

50. John 14:6, 17:3, 17:17; Romans 3:4; Titus 1:2; Hebrews 6:18.

51. Psalm 19:9, Revelation 19:1–2.

52. Romans 2:4; 1 Timothy 1:16; 1 Peter 3:20; 2 Peter 3:9, 3:15.

"some irrational passion bursting forth uncontrollably, but a burning zeal for the right coupled with a perfect hatred for everything that is evil."[53]

Putting It Together

According to this fifth model, God does not *suspend* one attribute (love or mercy) in order to exercise another attribute (judgment or wrath). Rather God's attributes work in harmony with each other. This does not mean that each of God's attributes is *equally* displayed in each of God's actions. In some of God's actions we may get a clearer glimpse of his wrath, in others his love, or his power, wisdom, patience, etc. But according to this last model which I endorse, all of God's attributes act in unison with each other, rather than competing or conflicting with one another. As one theologian said, "God is a unity and everything he does is an act of the whole person of God."[54]

In summary, our final model contends that God's love and wrath are both vital aspects of his character. Like the sparkling facets of a diamond, these two attributes are distinct but united. Neither can be reduced to the other, but they should be kept together. Christians affirm that Jesus' humanity and divinity are distinct natures that work together harmoniously in one united person, though we may not always understand how. We can also affirm that love and wrath work together harmoniously in one united God, though we may not always understand how. We want to grasp and treasure everything that God has revealed to be true of himself, and this includes both the love and wrath that flow out of who God is. But at the same time we also want to acknowledge that we are far, far from grasping the fullness of who God is—which is the final point of this chapter.

A MODEL IS JUST A MODEL

I have presented the fifth model as an improvement upon the other four. I believe it does a better job than the others of "avoiding the ditches" and

53. Morris, *Apostolic Preaching of the Cross*, 181.

54. Grudem, *Systematic Theology*, 180. See also Tony Lane's helpful statement: "There is no dichotomy in God's being between his mercy and his wrath, but there is a clear dichotomy between them in the way that they encounter us. Bernard [a famous twelfth-century Christian leader] was justified therefore in describing mercy and judgment as the two feet of God. They are feet that are united in the single person of their owner but that we encounter to some extent separately" ("Wrath of God as an Aspect of the Love of God," 146).

keeping us on "the road of truth." At the same time, I want to acknowledge that, like any model, it is far from perfect. I endorse the fifth model because I think it helps us understand our great God, but I realize that, like the others, this model is a limited human attempt to comprehend the incomprehensible God as best we can. All of our theology on this side of heaven is provisional, and it will surely be corrected and enriched in the life to come. In Paul's famous words, "now we see but a poor reflection in a mirror; then we shall see face to face. Now I know in part; then I shall know fully, even as I am fully known."[55]

One obstacle to our knowledge of God is our finite nature. We finite creatures cannot fully know God, who is infinite. The Psalmist exclaims, "Great is the LORD and most worthy of praise; his greatness no one can fathom." The apostle Paul cries out, "Oh, the depth of the riches of the wisdom and knowledge of God! How unsearchable his judgments, and his paths beyond tracing out! 'Who has known the mind of the Lord? Or who has been his counselor?'"[56] Due to our human limits, God remains well beyond our comprehension. We should never presume to have God all figured out. Far from it!

Sin is a second obstacle to our knowledge of God. The Bible teaches that apart from the renewing work of the Holy Spirit, the fallen human mind is hostile and blind to spiritual truth. While sin may not have any obvious effects on our knowledge of math, it definitely distorts our knowledge of God. That is why we sinners need to have our minds renewed in Christ. The presence of sin in our lives, individually and corporately, is a major barrier to our knowledge of God. We can overcome this barrier partially in this life by progressive sanctification (increasing in holiness and decreasing in sin), but sin will continue to cloud our knowledge of God until we are glorified in heaven.[57]

Does this mean that we will never know anything about God and must toss up our hands in despair? No. God has revealed himself to us in creation, in his mighty acts through history, in Scripture, and in his Son. So we are not simply left adrift in trying to understand God. According to the book of 1 John, we can know that God is light and that God is love.

---

55. 1 Corinthians 13:12.

56. Psalm 145:3, Romans 11:33–34.

57. Romans 1:18, 12:2; 1 Corinthians 2:14; 2 Corinthians 4:4; Ephesians 4:17–18, 4:23–4; Colossians 1:21. For a thorough examination of this topic, see Moroney, *Noetic Effects of Sin.*

And beyond knowing *about God*, by his grace, we can actually *know God himself*! John concludes his first letter by saying, "we know also that the Son of God has come and has given us understanding, so that we may know him who is true."[58]

The point of this last section is simply to remind us of our limitations. The fifth model surely flirts with and perhaps falls into ditches of its own—which critics will certainly point out! As one theologian said, "it is clear that no one explanation can contain all that might be said about a God of love who is also an angry God."[59] The fifth model proposed in this chapter is not the final word on the subject of God's love and God's wrath. It is merely an attempt to avoid some problems of earlier models in hopes of moving us toward a more adequate (or less inadequate!) understanding of how God's love relates to God's wrath. As noted in chapter two, rather than being discouraged that we cannot grasp God's character exhaustively, we can see this as an exciting, endless adventure. Throughout our lives we can continually grow in the knowledge of God.

This chapter (and this whole book) is written in the spirit of Paul's prayer for the Ephesians: "I keep asking that the God of our Lord Jesus Christ, the glorious Father, may give you the Spirit of wisdom and revelation, *so that you may know him better.*" God's people want to know our Lord to the fullest extent possible, while also remaining humble in the realization that all of our theological constructions are provisional. While we can enjoy a true but partial knowledge of God in this life, the full hope of God's people is oriented to the future. In the words of the apostle John, "We know that when he [Jesus] appears, we shall be like him, for we shall see him as he is."[60] What a day that will be!

CONCLUSION

This chapter has continued to make the case that God's love and judgment belong together. We should cherish both of these attributes because they are expressions of God's multifaceted and united character. Both love and wrath (a manifestation of God's judgment against sin) flow out of who God is. They reveal distinct aspects of God's character but should not be pitted against each other. Various models offer partial explanations of the

58. 1 John 1:5, 4:8, 4:16. The final quote is from 1 John 5:20.

59. Campbell, *Gospel of Anger*, 10. See also comments on page 107.

60. Ephesians 1:17, 1 John 3:2. See also Paul's related prayer in Colossians 1:10.

relationship between God's love and wrath. I favor the model that says God's love and wrath work together harmoniously, both flowing out of God's very nature, though we certainly do not understand all of God's ways. This model, like others, is an effort to understand, as best we can, the glorious God who is far beyond our full comprehension. So, like all theological models, it will certainly be corrected and improved upon by others.

By now, some readers' heads are probably spinning with all this theology. Those who are practically oriented want to know what difference all of this makes for our daily lives. The final chapter of this book will help draw connections between our view of God and the nitty-gritty of our lives. The main idea is that just as we should keep love and judgment together in our understanding of God, we also need to incorporate both elements in our own lives. Since we are called to be imitators of God and to reflect God's image to others, these two attributes of love and judgment should be displayed in our relationships with others. This is challenging since most of us are more comfortable with the idea of reflecting God's love than we are with reflecting God's judgment. It will be the burden of the final chapter to show that as God transforms his people increasingly into the image of Jesus Christ, both godly love and godly judgment should flow out of who we are—at the right times, in the right ways, in response to the right situations.

Questions for Reflection and Discussion

1. Can we really *cherish* God's judgment like we cherish God's love? Explain.

2. Do you agree that model #1 and model #2 slip off the "road of truth" and into some "dangerous ditches"? What are the most serious "ditches" we need to watch out for?

3. In your view, where do models #3 and #4 get it right and where do they get it wrong?

4. Argue *for or against* the idea that "love and wrath are both expressions of the very nature of God so that ultimately God's love and wrath work together harmoniously."

5. What is your response (discouraged, humbled, excited, awed, or something else) when you consider that God is not fully comprehensible to us, as finite and fallen creatures?

6

How Should We Live?

Reflecting Love and Judgment Together as God-Imagers

THE FIRST TWO PARTS of this book highlighted problems with believing in a God who judges without loving or who loves without
judging. Thus far, part three of the book has attempted to join love and
judgment together in our understanding of God. The previous chapter
argued that God's love and judgment should both be cherished as expressions of God's very nature. That is, God's love and God's judgment both
flow out of *who God is*.

If this understanding of God is accurate, then we would expect to
find displays of both love and judgment when the Son of God became human and lived among us. And that is exactly what we find in the first half
of this chapter when we survey the life and ministry of Jesus, as reported
in the Gospel of Matthew.

But love and judgment are not just for Jesus. They are traits Jesus'
followers are supposed to exhibit in our lives as well. So, the second half of
the chapter explores some practical ways we can join love and judgment
together in our day-to-day relationships.

LOVE AND JUDGMENT IN JESUS' MINISTRY (SURVEY
OF THE GOSPEL OF MATTHEW)

Jesus Christ, God in the flesh, showed amazing love for people *and* warned
people over and over of a cataclysmic judgment to come. Though Mark,
Luke, and John have much to say about this subject, to keep it simple we
will survey only the Gospel of Matthew. It is striking to see the constant
toggling back and forth between love and judgment. Matthew offers the
following summary of Jesus' early ministry (4:23–24):

> ²³Jesus went throughout Galilee, teaching in their synagogues, preaching the good news of the kingdom, and healing every disease and sickness among the people. ²⁴News about him spread all over Syria, and people brought to him all who were ill with various diseases, those suffering severe pain, the demon-possessed, those having seizures, and the paralyzed, and he healed them.

The people needed to be instructed in God's ways; so Jesus taught in their synagogues. They needed to hear the gospel; so Jesus preached the good news of the kingdom. They needed to be cured of their ailments; so Jesus healed every disease and sickness among them. Jesus gave and gave and gave some more. *Surely we can see a heart of love in Jesus' tireless ministry to others—hour after hour, day after day.*

But we also hear firm warnings flowing from the lips of Jesus (5:27–30):

> ²⁷You have heard that it was said, "Do not commit adultery." ²⁸But I tell you that anyone who looks at a woman lustfully has already committed adultery with her in his heart. ²⁹If your right eye causes you to sin, gouge it out and throw it away. It is better for you to lose one part of your body than for your whole body to be thrown into hell. ³⁰And if your right hand causes you to sin, cut it off and throw it away. It is better for you to lose one part of your body than for your whole body to go into hell.

Jesus announced that God's standards for holiness were much higher than commonly thought. God did not want people merely to avoid unfaithful sexual acts, but to avoid even lustful looks. He taught that sin requires radical surgery and he encouraged people to take drastic measures in cutting sin out of their lives—a point he reinforced later also (18:8–9). *Jesus warned, do whatever it takes to avoid going to hell.*

Jesus also called his followers to a radical love that is hard to live out (5:43–46):

> ⁴³You have heard that it was said, "Love your neighbor and hate your enemy." ⁴⁴But I tell you: Love your enemies and pray for those who persecute you, ⁴⁵that you may be sons of your Father in heaven. He causes his sun to rise on the evil and the good, and sends rain on the righteous and the unrighteous. ⁴⁶If you love those who love you, what reward will you get? Are not even the tax collectors doing that?

It is natural to love those who love us. Even people with bad reputa-tions (corrupt tax collectors) love those who love them. But if we are going to imitate God's character, then we are called to the supernatural standard of loving our enemies. God shows kindness to all people—providing sunshine and rain not only for the good/righteous but also for the evil/unrighteous. Jesus himself died for those who hated him. While hanging on the cross Jesus prayed for his executioners, "Father, forgive them, for they do not know what they are doing." In the same way, Jesus' followers are called to love their enemies and to pray for their persecutors.[1] *Jesus' love is definitely a radical love!*

Radical love is followed by radical warnings of spiritual danger (7:13–15, 21–23):

> [13]Enter through the narrow gate. For wide is the gate and broad is the road that leads to destruction, and many enter through it. [14]But small is the gate and narrow the road that leads to life, and only a few find it. [15]Watch out for false prophets. They come to you in sheep's clothing but inwardly they are ferocious wolves. . . . [21]Not everyone who says to me, "Lord, Lord," will enter the kingdom of heaven, but only he who does the will of my Father who is in heaven. [22]Many will say to me on that day, "Lord, Lord, did we not prophesy in your name, and in your name drive out demons and perform many miracles?" [23]Then I will tell them plainly, "I never knew you. Away from me, you evildoers!"

Unlike many today (see chapters three and four), Jesus warned peo-ple of spiritual landmines to be avoided. There is a *wide* gate and *broad* road that leads to *destruction*, which *many* find, in contrast to the *small* gate and *narrow* road that leads to *life*, which only a *few* find. To avoid the roomy road to destruction, Jesus warned his followers to watch out for false prophets who are not what they appear to be, but actually lead people astray. It is not enough for a person to address Jesus as Lord or claim to have done miraculous activity in his name. As one commentator said, "Jesus presents *himself* as the judge" and "the criterion of judgment is their relationship with *him*."[2] *On that day, the day of final judgment, Jesus will identify those who truly know him and those who do not.*

---

1. Luke 23:34, Acts 7:59–60, 1 Corinthians 4:12–13. See also the related admonition in 1 Peter 3:9.

2. France, *Gospel According to Matthew*, 149 (italics in the original). Travis concurs that "relation to Christ, then, is the criterion of judgement" (*Christ and the Judgement of God*, 325).

The Gospel of Matthew then reports Jesus' love in action through healing a man with leprosy (8:1–4), a centurion's servant (8:5–13), Peter's mother-in-law (8:14–15), two demon-possessed men (8:28–34), a paralytic (9:1–8), a sick woman, a dead girl, a blind man, and a mute man (9:18–33). When Jesus "saw the crowds, he had compassion on them, because they were harassed and helpless, like sheep without a shepherd" (9:36). Because of his loving nature, Jesus had a deep concern for those who were lost and hurting; so he multiplied his ministry of love by sending out the twelve disciples with his authority to preach that "'the kingdom of heaven is near.' Heal the sick, raise the dead, cleanse those who have leprosy, drive out demons" (10:8). *Jesus trained his disciples to follow his example in carrying out a practical ministry of love.*

At the same time, Jesus' ministry of love was coupled with severe warnings of coming judgment for those who did not repent (11:20–24):

> [20]"Then Jesus began to denounce the cities in which most of his miracles had been performed, because they did not repent. [21]"Woe to you, Korazin! Woe to you, Bethsaida! If the miracles that were performed in you had been performed in Tyre and Sidon, they would have repented long ago in sackcloth and ashes. [22]But I tell you, it will be more bearable for Tyre and Sidon on the day of judgment than for you. [23]And you, Capernaum, will you be lifted up to the skies? No, you will go down to the depths. If the miracles that were performed in you had been performed in Sodom, it would have remained to this day. [24]But I tell you that it will be more bearable for Sodom on the day of judgment than for you.

These cities should have recognized that God was powerfully at work in Jesus' miracles and they should have repented from their sins. Even the notorious pagan cities of Tyre, Sidon, and Sodom would have responded more positively to Jesus than these Galilean towns! As Jesus said later, "the men of Nineveh will stand up at the judgment with this generation and condemn it; for they repented at the preaching of Jonah, and now one greater than Jonah is here" (12:41). So, Matthew reports, Jesus "regularly told his listeners to fear those things worth fearing—especially the judgment of God."[3] *Jesus warned those who heard his preaching but who did not repent that judgment day was coming.*

While Jesus afflicted the comfortable with stern words of judgment, he also comforted the afflicted with tender words of mercy (11:28–30): "Come

---

3. Galli, *Jesus Mean and Wild*, 155.

to me, all you who are weary and burdened, and I will give you rest. Take my yoke upon you and learn from me, for I am gentle and humble in heart, and you will find rest for your souls. For my yoke is easy and my burden is light." In contrast to the scribes and Pharisees who laid heavy loads on the people by their interpretations and additions to the law (23:4), Jesus came to bring relief to the weary and burdened. He made demands of his disciples, but Jesus' yoke was easy and his burden was light, perhaps because when Jesus asked something of his followers, he also provided them with all they needed to live it out. *What Christ's commands required, his grace supplied.*

This grace enjoyed by Jesus' followers, however, comes into sharp relief when it is contrasted with the fiery judgment that awaits those who follow the evil one. Matthew reports that Jesus explained his parable of the weeds with these words (13:37–43):

> [37]The one who sowed the good seed is the Son of Man. [38]The field is the world, and the good seed stands for the sons of the kingdom. The weeds are the sons of the evil one, [39]and the enemy who sows them is the devil. The harvest is the end of the age, and the harvest-ers are angels. [40]As the weeds are pulled up and burned in the fire, so it will be at the end of the age. [41]The Son of Man will send out his angels, and they will weed out of his kingdom everything that causes sin and all who do evil. [42]They will throw them into the fiery furnace, where there will be weeping and gnashing of teeth. [43]Then the righteous will shine like the sun in the kingdom of their Father. He who has ears, let him hear.

One of Jesus' central points in the parable (13:24–30) was that "God endures the wicked in the present to provide all those who will receive him time to become his followers."[4] At the same time, Jesus was crystal clear that at the end of the age the Son of Man will send out angels to sift humans into two groups: (1) those who cause sin and do evil—who will be thrown into the fiery furnace and (2) the righteous—who will shine like the sun in their Father's kingdom. Jesus reinforced this point when he explained the parable of the net (13:49–50): "This is how it will be at the end of the age. The angels will come and separate the wicked from the righteous and throw them into the fiery furnace where there will be weeping and gnashing of teeth." *In the end, Jesus said, the wicked and the righteous will be separated and the wicked will suffer a fiery ordeal.*

4. Keener, *Matthew*, 244.

At the same time, Jesus showed his power and love by feeding huge crowds of thousands (14:13–21, 15:29–38). Jesus healed suffering girls and boys (15:21–28, 17:14–18). He taught his followers to forgive each other from the heart and to show mercy to each other (18:21–35). In fact, Jesus taught that God is so incredibly generous toward the undeserving that we must be careful not to be envious when others receive a lavish dose of God's grace (20:1–16). When people cried out to Jesus for mercy, his very nature was to have compassion on them (20:29–34). *According to Jesus, all the law and the prophets hang on the two commandments to love God and love neighbor* (22:34–40).

These themes of forgiveness, mercy, grace, and love are set right alongside other themes of judgment. Jesus forcefully cleared the temple to restore its intended purpose as a house of prayer (21:12–17). He told the chief priests and elders, "the kingdom of God will be taken away from you and given to a people who will produce its fruit" (21:43). His parables showed that those outside the kingdom of heaven will be thrown out in "the darkness, where there will be weeping and gnashing of teeth" (22:13). Jesus pronounced woes against the teachers of the law and Pharisees, in strikingly harsh language (23:13–36). He said that at his return those who were disobedient and those who were foolishly unprepared would be left out of the kingdom of heaven, banished to a place where there will be weeping and gnashing of teeth—a picture of regret and anguish (24:45—25:30). *When the Son of Man comes in his glory, Jesus said, he will separate people into two groups—one going away to eternal punishment and the other to eternal life (25:31–46).*

This eternal life, of course, was made possible by Jesus' loving death in the place of sinners. Jesus spoke of his mission to "give his life as a ransom for many" (20:28). Even when he was "overwhelmed with sorrow to the point of death" in Gethsemane, Jesus prayerfully submitted his will to the Father's will (26:36–44). Rather than calling on thousands of angels to deliver him, Jesus fulfilled God's plan for him by allowing his arrest (26:47–56). When challenged to save himself from crucifixion, instead *Jesus lovingly and obediently stayed up on the cross in order to save others, even though it meant that he would have to endure the experience of God-forsakenness* (27:39–50).

In sum, Matthew gives us a rich account of *both love and judgment* in Jesus' ministry. Jesus expressed love mostly through immediate actions, while speaking of judgment mainly through warnings about the future. When God lived among us in the flesh, his attributes of love and judgment were displayed in such an intertwined way that they cannot be disentangled without doing violence to the gospel (Jefferson's scissors). Jesus is "both friend of sinners and righteous Judge, extending both mercy and wrath. Jesus is surprising and unpredictable; he is faithful, demanding, chastising and rebuking, yet loving. In his person and his actions, Jesus is complex."[5] Too often our images of Christ are simple and one-sided rather than complex and multi-sided. We simplify Jesus by ignoring the parts that we may not like. But if we dare to be honest, we must affirm that "the Jesus of the New Testament, who is the world's Savior, is its Judge as well."[6]

JUDGE NOT?

I hope that by this point in the book, most readers are convinced that it is a huge mistake to separate God's love from God's judgment. Whether in the Old Testament or in the New Testament (when God's Son walked among us), God has revealed himself to be a God of love *and* a God of judgment. Fair enough, but in our lives as humans aren't we called to love and not to judge? Aren't we supposed to imitate God's love but not God's judgment? Many readers probably object to the whole notion of *human* judging because Jesus told us not to do it. In this section I offer a brief interpretation of what Jesus did and did not mean in his famous statement, recorded in Matthew 7:1–5:

> [1]Do not judge, or you too will be judged. [2]For in the same way you judge others, you will be judged, and with the measure you use, it will be measured to you. [3]Why do you look at the speck of sawdust in your brother's eye and pay no attention to the plank in your own eye? [4]How can you say to your brother, "Let me take the speck out of your eye," when all the time there is a plank in your own eye? [5]You hypocrite, first take the plank out of your own eye, and then you will see clearly to remove the speck from your brother's eye.

There is no doubt that Jesus spoke out against a certain type of judging here. Specifically, Jesus seemed to be "concerned with the fault-finding, condemnatory attitude which is too often combined with a blindness to one's own failings." A key problem with the hypocrite here is "his failure to

---

5. Nichols, *Jesus Made in America*, 226. See also the related comments on page 88.
6. Packer, *Knowing God*, 141.

apply to himself the criticism he so meticulously applies to his brother."[7] Imagine an ophthalmologist with big, blinding cataracts who tried to perform eye surgery on patients with minor impediments. We would tell the doctor to take care of his or her own issues before worrying about others' little problems.

Too often we are like that doctor. Most of us have a tendency to notice (or even search for!) small faults in others while excusing or overlooking huge faults in ourselves. Why do we so easily fall into this trap? One author offers the following explanation.

> Few activities in life rival the thrill of passing judgment on another human being. I don't believe I can go a day on God's green earth without in some way indulging in this forbidden art. . . . I pick up the newspaper in the morning (after condemning the paperboy for throwing it so that half the front page is torn) and find it full of people I can judge as being sinful, ignorant, stupid, arrogant, or childish. Lumping large groups of people together and at once dispatching the whole lot of them is especially effective. . . . The act of judging gives us a subjective means of affirming ourselves. No matter what I've done or how bad I am, I can always comfort myself by finding someone out there who is "worse" than I am. I can also bring down those who appear to be more worthy than me by finding or manufacturing some flaw in their character that allows me to be better than they are in my mind. . . . It's a foolproof way to feel good about ourselves.[8]

Ouch. Too often, that's me, trying to build myself up by tearing someone else down, even if it is only in my mind. And I know that when Christians have a hypocritical, self-righteous, judgmental spirit toward others, it is a huge turn-off.[9] We need to take Jesus seriously and quit searching for specks in others' eyes when we have huge planks in our own. We all live in glass houses and need to avoid throwing stones at others. But does that mean we can never make judgments of right and wrong?

---

7. The quotes in this paragraph are from France, *Gospel According to Matthew*, 142–43.

8. Fischer, *12 Steps for the Recovering Pharisee (Like Me)*, 14, 16, 18.

9. A recent study of 16- to 29-year olds found the two most common negative perceptions of present-day Christianity were that it was judgmental (87%) and hypocritical (85%). These results are reported in the Barna update of September 24, 2007 at http://www.barna.org/barna-update/article/16-teensnext-gen/94.

I agree with the theologian who said we should embrace "a worthy and biblical reticence in passing judgment on individuals" but not confuse this with "an unwillingness to make moral judgments to distinguish between what is morally good and what is evil."[10] Jesus forbids hypocritical *judgmentalism*, in which we self-righteously look down on others, but he does not ban judgment in the sense of exercising *moral discernment*. As one thinker said, "judgment is an act of *moral discrimination*, dividing right from wrong."[11] That sort of discerning judgment is a necessary part of following Jesus.

Jesus cannot have been ruling out all judging, unless his instructions recorded in Matthew 7 were completely at odds with what he said at other times. After all, later in his Gospel, Matthew records Jesus' instructions on how to handle sin in another believer. This process of church discipline requires *moral judgment* and confrontation of sin, but *not haughty judgmentalism* of looking down at others (18:15–17):

> [15]If your brother sins against you, go and show him his fault, just between the two of you. If he listens to you, you have won your brother over. [16]But if he will not listen, take one or two others along, so that every matter may be established by the testimony of two or three witnesses. [17]If he refuses to listen to them, tell it to the church; and if he refuses to listen even to the church, treat him as you would a pagan or a tax collector.

Along similar lines, John's Gospel reports a disagreement Jesus had with a group in Jerusalem. The Jewish leaders accepted that a child could be circumcised on the Sabbath to keep the law of Moses. So, Jesus asked, "why are you angry with me for healing the whole man [or making a man completely well] on the Sabbath?" (7:23). Jesus pointed out, "if circumcising on the eighth day takes precedence over the Sabbath . . . , saving a whole life also does."[12] These leaders were not reasoning rightly. So Jesus told them to "stop judging by mere appearances and make a right judgment" (7:24). Jesus' antidote to engaging in wrong judgment was to "judge

---

10. Lane, "Wrath of God as an Aspect of the Love of God," 157.

11. O'Donovan, *Ways of Judgment*, 7. Morris agrees that in its normal Old Testament use (the word *shaphat*), "basically judgment is the process whereby one discerns between the right and the wrong *and takes action as a result*" (*Biblical Doctrine of Judgment*, 17).

12. Keener, *IVP Bible Background Commentary: New Testament*, 282.

with right judgment."[13] Since Jesus said it, there must be a proper way for people to judge rightly.

The Bible teaches that humans were created in God's image and likeness.[14] And as we have seen, God is a God of love *and* judgment. Christians are further called to be like Christ,[15] and as we have seen, Christ's ministry included both love *and* judgment. The question then naturally arises: are there some ways that God's people are called to reflect God's character by joining love and judgment together in our own lives?

I believe that as God makes us more like himself, both love and judgment can flow out of us in godly ways. Some aspects of judgment are properly left to God alone. We will never be God. But as faint and imperfect images of God, there is a place for love and judgment in our lives. The rest of this chapter explores three ways we can reflect God's image by keeping love and judgment together in our relationships with each other.

REFLECTING GOD'S LOVE AND JUDGMENT TOGETHER IN DISCIPLINARY CORRECTION

God's Disciplinary Correction

The book of Proverbs teaches us that God's discipline, which might appear to be simply an instance of judgment, actually includes an element of God's love also. "My son, do not despise the LORD's discipline and do not resent his rebuke, because the LORD disciplines those he loves, as a father the son he delights in" (3:11–12). We can see God's love and judgment acting together when God disciplines the nation of Israel.

Deuteronomy 8 opens by recounting how God used the forty years of wandering in the desert to discipline Israel for its earlier failures. We are told that God "humbled you, causing you to hunger and then feeding you with manna, which neither you nor your fathers had known, to teach you that man does not live on bread alone but on every word that comes from the mouth of God" (8:3). The Israelites were cautioned to "know then in your heart that as a man disciplines his son, so the LORD your God disciplines you" (8:5).

---

13. The same Greek word (*krinō*) is used for "judge" in Matthew 7:1 (do not judge) and John 7:24 (judge with right judgment).

14. Genesis 1:26–27, 5:3, 9:6.

15. Romans 8:29, 1 Corinthians 15:49, 2 Corinthians 3:18.

The Old Testament compares God's disciplinary correction of those he loves with our human disciplinary correction of those we love. The New Testament extends this lesson even further, when the author of Hebrews quotes Proverbs 3:11–12 as a "word of encouragement" (12:5–6) and then adds the following exhortation (12:7–11):

> [7]Endure hardship as discipline; God is treating you as sons. For what son is not disciplined by his father? [8]If you are not disciplined (and everyone undergoes discipline), then you are illegitimate children and not true sons. [9]Moreover, we have all had human fathers who disciplined us and we respected them for it. How much more should we submit to the Father of our spirits and live! [10]Our fathers disciplined us for a little while as they thought best; but God disciplines us for our good, that we may share in his holiness. [11]No discipline seems pleasant at the time, but painful. Later on, however, it produces a harvest of righteousness and peace for those who have been trained by it.

Most children undergo some sort of discipline and we usually respect our parents for it, assuming they were doing what they thought best. So how much more should we recognize that God disciplines us for our good, that we may share in his holiness? God's discipline produces righteousness and peace for those who have been trained by it. As the Psalmist said, "before I was afflicted I went astray, but now I obey your word . . . it was good for me to be afflicted so that I might learn your decrees . . . and in faithfulness you have afflicted me" (119:67, 71, 75). Such wisdom helps God's children realize that God is neither an all-accepting, indulgent grandparent nor a gleefully punitive police officer, but rather a perfect heavenly Father.

Human Disciplinary Correction

We are called to follow God's model by demonstrating both judgment and love in our discipline. When we refuse to make judgments of right and wrong and correct our children accordingly, we fail to train them in godliness. It is a pity that some parents, for a variety of reasons, fail to discipline their children. Undisciplined children often walk very hard roads as adults. Proverbs 13:24 says, "he who spares the rod hates his son, but he who loves him is careful to discipline him." It is also a pity that some parents do not discipline their children out of love, but out of harshness. Harshly disciplined children also walk hard roads as adults, which is why Scripture warns fathers to "not exasperate your children" and to "not embitter your children, or they will become discouraged."[16]

We parents mess up all the time. But sometimes, just sometimes, by God's grace, we get it right in our parenting. We keep love and judgment together and they flow out of us in just the right way at just the right time. We pray and aspire to times like these, when a spouse can see God working in us: "One of my husband's finer moments in parenting came one day when, after he had uttered an unwelcome word of correction to a disgruntled child, he leaned down, looked her in the eye, and said, 'Honey, this is what love looks like.'"[17] Wise judgment and warm love combine for godly parental discipline.

The same is true with church discipline. Scripture indicates that when sins such as divisiveness, incest, and blasphemy are publicly evident and persistent over time,[18] the church is called to lovingly confront the one caught in a pattern of sin.[19] This should be done as unobtrusively as possible at first and always with a spirit of gentleness.[20] The desired outcome is that the person entrapped in sin will repent.[21] The aim of church discipline is to restore erring brothers or sisters,[22] and also to encourage holy living.[23]

All too often, in contemporary American churches, discipline is not administered when it should be. It is sad when a person wanders away from the truth and his or her church fails to call him or her to repentance. James says, "whoever turns a sinner from the error of his way will save him from death and cover over a multitude of sins" (5:20). Likewise it is a sad when a person is subjected to church discipline that is administered for a wrong reason or in a wrong way, violating biblical standards and leaving deep scars.

Churches mess up all the time by failing to render proper judgments and by failing to do so from a motive of love. But again sometimes, just sometimes, by God's grace, churches get it right. It *is* humanly possible

16. Ephesians 6:4 and Colossians 3:21.

17. McEntyre, "Nice is Not the Point," 104.

18. Romans 16:17, Titus 3:10, 1 Corinthians 5:1, and 1 Timothy 1:20.

19. Matthew 18:15–17, 1 Corinthians 5:1–13, and Galatians 6:1.

20. Matthew 18:15, Galatians 6:1.

21. 2 Corinthians 7:10.

22. Matthew 18:15, Galatians 6:1, 1 Timothy 1:20, and James 5:19–20.

23. 1 Corinthians 5:1–7, 1 Timothy 1:20, and Revelation 2:20.

to keep love and judgment together in the right way in response to the right situation. In 1 Corinthians 5, Paul said of a man who was sexually involved with his father's wife (perhaps his stepmother), "I have already passed judgment on the one who did this, just as if I were present" (5:3). Paul did not judge the sexually immoral "people of this world" who did not follow Jesus (5:9–10). But within the church, there is a place for discipline guided by loving judgment. That is why Paul asked, rhetorically, "what business is it of mine to judge those outside the church? Are you not to judge those inside? God will judge those outside" (5:12–13).

The good news is the Corinthians apparently did learn to exercise proper church discipline; so in 2 Corinthians Paul gave them follow-up instructions on how to wrap up the matter.[24] Since the punishment had been sufficient, Paul urged the Corinthians not to continue the discipline but rather to forgive and comfort the restored brother, so he would not be overwhelmed by excessive sorrow (2:6–7).[25] Paul then urged the Corinthians to reaffirm their love for the repentant one (2:8). Good parents discipline their children, but when their children express true sorrow and repentance, the parents immediately reassure the children that they are forgiven and loved. By analogy, the repentant brother in Corinth needed to be reassured of the congregation's love for him, perhaps by a public reaffirmation of their corporate love for him. Again, love and judgment belong together.

As one scholar said, "without some form of church discipline, which inevitably involves some kind of judging, the church becomes merely

---

24. Some commentators speculate that the person referred to in 2 Corinthians 2 was the individual discussed earlier in 1 Corinthians 5, who was living in immorality. If this view is correct, then Paul was indicating that the church did in fact carry out the punishment of "expelling" or "not associating" with this man, but since he had repented they were to forgive and reaffirm their love for him (2 Corinthians 2:6–7). Other commentators speculate that the person referred to in 2 Corinthians 2 was someone who, during Paul's "painful/sorrowful visit" publicly challenged Paul's apostolic authority by demanding proof that Christ was speaking through Paul (2 Corinthians 13:2–3). If this view is correct, then Paul was indicating that in accordance with his test of obedience (2 Corinthians 2:9), the church at Corinth had stood up for Paul and inflicted some sort of punishment on this person which had brought about his repentance. Paul had forgiven him; so that the church should forgive him also. In either of these scenarios, it is clear that the Corinthians had rightly exercised church discipline on the offending member.

25. Unlike the customs of the Essenes and Greco-Roman law, Paul did not insist that a required time of punishment elapse prior to full restoration.

a social club without real meaning or purpose."[26] However, when done rightly, this judging is not "judgmental" or self-righteous. Instead it is a godly judgment that looks out for what is best for others. Healthy discipline is truly a sign of love—whether from God to believers, from parents to children, or from the church to its members. When we carry out discipline properly, we join judgment and love together, thereby bearing God's image, in which we were created.

REFLECTING GOD'S LOVE AND JUDGMENT TOGETHER IN RIGHTEOUS ANGER

Righteous Anger in Jesus' Ministry

Jesus, God in the flesh, exhibited righteous anger on a number of occasions, as seen in the Gospel of Mark. Early on, Mark reports the following incident (3:1–6):

> [1]Another time he went into the synagogue, and a man with a shriveled hand was there. [2]Some of them were looking for a reason to accuse Jesus, so they watched him closely to see if he would heal him on the Sabbath. [3]Jesus said to the man with the shriveled hand, 'Stand up in front of everyone.' [4]Then Jesus asked them, 'Which is lawful on the Sabbath: to do good or to do evil, to save life or to kill?' But they remained silent. [5]He looked around at them in anger and, deeply distressed at their stubborn hearts, said to the man, 'Stretch out your hand.' He stretched it out, and his hand was completely restored. [6]Then the Pharisees went out and began to plot with the Herodians how they might kill Jesus.

The Pharisees here were more concerned with their understanding of Sabbath-keeping than they were with doing good or saving lives. And *Jesus cared* that these leaders *did not care* for what was really *worth caring about*. The way they put their regulations above the pressing human need right in front of them made Jesus angry—righteously angry.

Later in the Gospel of Mark we find another report of Jesus being angry at people's misplaced priorities, though this time the culprits were not the Pharisees, but Jesus' own disciples. Sometimes Jesus was angry with those closest to him (10:13–16):

---

26. Olson, *Questions to All Your Answers*, 168–69.

> [13]People were bringing little children to Jesus to have him touch them, but the disciples rebuked them. [14]When Jesus saw this, he was indignant. He said to them, 'Let the little children come to me, and do not hinder them, for the kingdom of God belongs to such as these. [15]I tell you the truth, anyone who will not receive the kingdom of God like a little child will never enter it.' [16]And he took the children in his arms, put his hands on them and blessed them.

Greek scholars note that the word that is "translated as 'indignant' means to feel irritated and annoyed, discontented, a word that clearly conveys Jesus' anger at his disciples."[27] Jesus was indignant because his disciples were trying to prevent people from bringing little children to him. Jesus wanted to take the young ones in his arms, place his hands on them and bless them. After all, the humble, open, receptive trust of these children was a perfect picture of how we must receive the kingdom of God.

The last instance of Jesus' anger in Mark is the most well known (11:15–17):

> [15]On reaching Jerusalem, Jesus entered the temple area and began driving out those who were buying and selling there. He overturned the tables of the money changers and the benches of those selling doves, [16]and would not allow anyone to carry merchandise through the temple courts. [17]And as he taught them, he said, 'Is it not written: "My house will be called a house of prayer for all nations"? But you have made it 'a den of robbers.'"

When Jesus arrived in Jerusalem, he found a bustling business in the temple. Historians tell us that it had been rather recently, within Jesus' lifetime, that the stalls of sacrificial animals had been moved into the court of the Gentiles—infringing on their worship and prayer there. Jesus drove all the merchants and animals out of the temple, where they did not belong. He also overturned the moneychangers' tables and would not allow people to carry merchandise through the temple courts. When he encountered something contrary to his Father's will, Jesus judged it to be wrong and took appropriate actions that showed his deep love and zeal for what God really wanted.[28] Jesus expressed righteous anger without ever letting it degenerate into a temper tantrum or fit of rage. As one

27. Lester, *Angry Christian*, 163.
28. On this, see the account found in John 2:16–17.

scholar observed, "from the life of Jesus, we can clearly see that anger and love work together."[29] Is that possible for us? Can we experience righteous anger in *our* lives?

Righteous Human Anger

As with discipline, so also with anger, we humans can fail to reflect God's image. *First, we can become angry about the wrong things.* God is angry with sin, but I'm often angry with more self-centered concerns—traffic that slows me down or a mechanical problem I can't fix (for me, that's most mechanical problems). Jesus' anger was not about himself. No anger is reported even when Peter denied him, Judas betrayed him, Pilate sentenced him, and the soldiers crucified him. Jesus' anger focused on wrongs being done to others. Jesus shows us that we often get mad at the wrong stuff.

Second, we can express our anger in ungodly ways. As one pastor observed, "even when we are angry about the right things, our own sinfulness usually pollutes our anger. . . . God's anger is pure and untainted by sin."[30] Human anger can be dangerous, which is why Scripture warns us again and again to be careful with it.[31] Jesus told his followers that "anyone who is angry with his brother will be subject to judgment."[32] The Greek word translated "who is angry" may be understood as denoting a continuous action. The New English Bible says, "whoever nurses anger against a brother will be liable to judgment," indicating excessively long, continual anger. As one expert said, "all of us know how easy sinning is when we are angry."[33] That is why we are admonished to be like God himself, that is, to be slow to become angry.[34]

Slow anger, however, is different than *no* anger. Some Christians think we should always "bottle it up for God."[35] But that's wrong. We fail to reflect God's image at times because we *don't* become angry at things

29. Chambers, "Biblical Theology of Godly Human Anger," 237.

30. MacArthur, Jr., *God*, 90, 94.

31. For example, see 2 Corinthians 12:20, Galatians 5:20, Ephesians 4:26–27, and Colossians 3:8.

32. Matthew 5:22.

33. Andrew D. Lester, *Angry Christian*, 148.

34. Proverbs 14:17, 14:29, 16:32, 19:11; James 1:19–20.

35. Campbell, *Gospel of Anger*, 29.

that anger God. Here, "*not being angry* at evil in all of its manifestations is sinful."[36] As one theologian put it: "in the face of blatant evil we should be indignant not tolerant, angry not apathetic."[37]

God's wrath demonstrates his intense hatred of sin and evil, and there is a sense in which God's people should share in his hatred of sin and evil. The wisdom of Proverbs declares, "to fear the LORD is to hate evil; I hate pride and arrogance, evil behavior and perverse speech." The Psalmist cries out boldly, "let those who love the LORD hate evil" and "indignation grips me because of the wicked." We should even *hate the evil we see in our own lives.* When the prophet Nathan told David about a man who committed a great injustice, "David burned with anger against the man" and when he realized that *he* was the man, David immediately said to Nathan, "I have sinned against the LORD."[38]

Put simply, loving God entails hating the evil that God hates. Moses was right to "burn with anger" at the Israelites' idolatry and rebellion against the Lord. Paul said to "hate what is evil; cling to what is good." [39] Ideally our human anger should join love and judgment together so we can reflect the image of our God who both loves and judges. Perhaps this was what the prophet Jeremiah experienced when he reacted to Judah's sin by declaring, "I am full of the wrath of the LORD, and I cannot hold it in" (6:11).

We humans often get it wrong with our anger. We are *not* angry when we should be; we *are* angry when we should not be; and we express our anger in the *wrong* ways. But by God's grace, we are also capable of expressing anger in the right way. The key is that "godly anger battles for the sake of godly causes whenever the time is right."[40]

We must strive to align ourselves with God's values, so that we are angry about the right things and express our anger in the right ways. Then and only then, "anger can give us the energy and the willingness to speak up, speak out, march, vote, protest, refuse to participate, resist evil, and

36. Lester, *Angry Christian*, 207 (italics in the original). See also the related comments on page 215.

37. Stott, *God's New Society*, 186.

38. Proverbs 8:13; Psalm 97:10, 119:53; and 2 Samuel 12.

39. Exodus 32:19–35, Numbers 16:1–40, Romans 12:9.

40. Chambers, "Biblical Theology of Godly Human Anger," 304.

blow the whistle. Anger provides courage."[41] That sort of courage helped Martin Luther King Jr. and others stand up and speak out against the sin of racism in the United States. We must affirm that "godly human anger is a God-given anger that burns in abhorrence of sin," which is why "godly human anger is necessary in the life of every Christian."[42] Godly human anger, though rare, shows us how *true judgment* of sin and *true love* for those oppressed by sin can *work together in harmony.*

REFLECTING GOD'S LOVE AND JUDGMENT TOGETHER IN CARING CONFRONTATION

Caring Confrontation in Jesus' Life

Our survey of the Gospel of Matthew earlier in the chapter showed that Jesus did not shy away from confrontation. He confronted evil spirits, human sin, mistaken views of God's law, false professions of faith, failure to repent at his preaching, and failure to reckon seriously with the final judgment. Without a doubt, though, his most famous confrontations came with the teachers of the law and Pharisees. The twenty-third chapter of Matthew is filled with these confrontations. Consider some selections (23:13–33):

> [13]Woe to you, teachers of the law and Pharisees, you hypocrites! You shut the kingdom of heaven in men's faces. You yourselves do not enter, nor will you let those enter who are trying to. . . . [15]You travel over land and sea to win a single convert, and when he becomes one, you make him twice as much a son of hell as you are. . . . [27]You are like whitewashed tombs, which look beautiful on the outside but on the inside are full of dead men's bones and everything unclean. [28]In the same way, on the outside you appear to people as righteous but on the inside you are full of hypocrisy and wickedness. . . . [33]You snakes! You brood of vipers! How will you escape being condemned to hell?

No doubt these are strong words of judgment, but might they also be words of love as well? One pastor observes that, "nothing demonstrates God's love more than the various warnings throughout the pages

---

41. Lester, *Angry Christian*, 193. Campbell concurs that "in the unsettling experience of anger at oppression we may find the words which are ours to speak" (*Gospel of Anger*, 102).

42. Chambers, "Biblical Theology of Godly Human Anger," 115–16.

of Scripture, urging sinners to flee from the wrath to come."[43] It is often said that the opposite of love is indifference, and Jesus is certainly not indifferent here! Perhaps Jesus "judges that at this point in his ministry, the clearest, cleanest way to tell them they have strayed far from the ways of God is to confront them publicly." At the very least, Jesus shows us that "sometimes brusque confrontation is necessary. To avoid it is essentially to say that Jesus got this wrong. And to refuse confrontation is also to refuse to love."[44]

Jesus lovingly confronted not only the Pharisees but also a rich young man who came to him. Mark's Gospel records the story in this way (10:17–23, italics added):

> [17]As Jesus started on his way, a man ran up to him and fell on his knees before him. "Good teacher," he asked, "what must I do to inherit eternal life?" [18]"Why do you call me good?" Jesus answered. "No one is good—except God alone. [19]You know the command-ments: 'Do not murder, do not commit adultery, do not steal, do not give false testimony, do not defraud, honor your father and mother.' [20]"Teacher," he declared, "all these I have kept since I was a boy." [21]*Jesus looked at him and loved him. "One thing you lack,"* he said. *"Go, sell everything you have and give to the poor, and you will have treasure in heaven. Then come follow me."* [22]At this the man's face fell. He went away sad, because he had great wealth. [23]Jesus looked around and said to his disciples, "How hard it is for the rich to enter the kingdom of God!"

Jesus directly confronted the main spiritual barrier this man had to overcome. Out of deep love for the man, Jesus pinpointed the major idol in the man's life, the one thing (or perhaps hundreds of "things") he need-ed to give up to follow Christ. Jesus made a correct judgment about what was holding this man back spiritually, and he offered a direct prescription to cure his disease of materialism—"Go, sell everything you have and give to the poor, and you will have treasure in heaven." Jesus wanted what was best for the man (eternal life, treasure in heaven). So Jesus *judged* the man's situation accurately and *lovingly* confronted his sin—by pointing out what was holding him back spiritually. Once more, we must ask, how can *we* imitate Jesus' perfect blend of love and judgment?

---

43. MacArthur, *Love of God*, 122.

44. The quotes in this paragraph are from Galli, *Jesus Mean and Wild*, 68, 75.

Caring Confrontation in Our Lives

I don't always hit the right mix of love and judgment when I confront others, but others have hit the mark with me. Though it occurred more than a quarter century ago, I remember my first experience with caring Christian confrontation like it was yesterday. I was sitting in a circle on the floor of a dorm room at Duke University with a half-dozen other students. We were studying the book of Romans together. Less than a year earlier I had committed my life to trusting Jesus as my Savior and following him as my Lord. I was very rough around the edges (and still am, by God's standards).

Probably the least holy part of my life in those days was my speech. In high school I had reaped high social rewards for my witty humor. When hanging out with friends, I had a knack for delivering sarcastic lines that made the group laugh. So, naturally, I continued this pattern in college. And usually my sarcasm brought about the results I desired. It even seemed to work with our Bible study group in the dorm. Except I wasn't sharp enough socially to pick up on the fact that the leader did not appreciate my witty interruptions as much as the others who laughed. The leader's name was John.

I let fly with one of my patented zingers and the predictable laughter followed. But John wasn't smiling—not frowning but not smiling. He said, "Let's stop for just a minute. Steve, I want to tell you something that I just learned in my Greek class. Recently we learned that the Greek word for flesh is 'sarx,' and that's related to the root of the word sarcastic. The word picture behind 'sarcasm' is cutting flesh. So next time you make a sarcastic remark, you can just picture yourself taking a sharp scalpel and cutting someone's flesh open. Okay, well, let's get back to verse fourteen."

The Bible study started back up, but I was the one who had been cut open. I knew that what John said was true and though the words may sound harsh, the tone with which he delivered them was loving enough that I could not dismiss them as malicious. They were words of caring confrontation which I needed to hear. That night I began to ask God to change my speech and make it more godly. Later I realized the issue went even deeper, to what was going on in my heart. Amazingly, within a matter of weeks I wasn't talking the way I used to. John's caring confrontation combined *judgment* (that my speech was distracting, harmful, and sinful) with *love* (in the way he said it and in his follow-up encouragement that I could change, with God's help). Though it hurt at the time, within a matter of days I was grateful that John had confronted me. I began to understand the meaning of Proverbs 27:6—"wounds from a friend can be trusted."

When done rightly, confrontation is a form of caring that encourages a person's growth. With a blend of judgment and love, confrontation can create a moment of truth that calls a person to be his or her best self, the new self that God intends. As Paul said to the Ephesians, "you were taught, with regard to your former way of life, to put off your old self, which is being corrupted by its deceitful desires; to be made new in the attitude of your minds; and to put on the new self, created to be like God in true righteousness and holiness" (4:22–24). That's what Jesus helped people do when he caringly confronted them, and by God's grace, that's what John helped me do.

Of course, we mess up in this area also. As with discipline and anger, we fail to confront people when we should confront them. Too often I chicken out and don't do for others what John did for me. (Is this a tacit agreement that I won't confront you, if you don't confront me?) Or we can confront people over the wrong issues or in the wrong ways. John did not come at me with broad, judgmental generalizations. Instead he identified my particular behavior pattern that had negative effects on others.

Then the ball was in my court. There is no guarantee that people will respond positively to caring confrontation, even when it is done perfectly. Remember, the rich young man did not repent on the spot and neither did I. Initially he and I went away sad. Sometimes it takes a while for the truth from a caring confrontation to sink in. To my shame, that's usually the way it is when my wife confronts me—no matter how well she does it. But when God directs the process, caring confrontation is one more way we can reflect God's image by joining love and judgment together in our human relationships.

CONCLUSION

We know what love and judgment should look like by gazing upon God, especially God-in-the-flesh: Jesus Christ. Our gaze reveals a God who loves and judges. We are then called to reflect God's image, however faintly and imperfectly, by keeping love and judgment together in our own lives. Though we often fail in the task of properly reflecting God's image to others, this final chapter has suggested three ways this might be done, through God's grace—by administering disciplinary correction, by expressing righteous anger, and by engaging in caring confrontation. As God transforms his people increasingly into the image of Jesus Christ, both love and judgment should flow out of who we are—at the right times, in the right ways, in response to the right situations. Love and judgment are united together in the very character of God, and when we are at our best, love and judgment are united together in godly ways within our lives as well.

Questions for Reflection and Discussion

1. As you read through the constant toggling back and forth between love and judgment in Jesus' ministry, *what passages or what points stood out the most to you?*

2. Why do you think it is so tempting for us to judge other people self-righteously? And what are the best *safeguards or defenses* to keep us from giving in to this temptation?

3. When have you seen *parental discipline or church discipline* done *well or poorly?*

4. With what do *you struggle the most*: getting angry about the wrong things, not getting angry when you should, or expressing your anger in ungodly ways?

5. Share a story from your life of an instance when someone (maybe a family member, a friend, or someone else) *caringly confronted* you. What can we learn from that story?

Conclusion

Nearly every book of the Bible contains themes of God's love and judgment. What are we to make of this? One option is to emphasize God's judgment at the expense of his love. But there are serious problems when we presume to declare "thus judgeth the Lord" every time something goes wrong in our world. It was obvious to Thomas Beard and many Puritans that when something bad happened, God must have been sending heavenly judgment for earthly sin. Positively, Beard and other Puritans did not downplay what Scripture says about God as judge, as many do today. Negatively, Beard and other Puritans were wrong to be as certain about God's judgments in current events (when God did not provide a definite interpretation of what happened) as they were about God's judgments in biblical events (when God did provide a definite interpretation). Religious leaders today continue to see God's judgment in current events—as with the terrorist attacks of 9/11 or Hurricane Katrina—but Scripture teaches that when we hazard our own guesses about God's judgments in the events of our times we are often mistaken.

Martin Luther shows us just how terrifying it can be to believe in a God of judgment who is not also a God of love. It is impossible for us to find spiritual peace when we are living in constant dread of God pictured as the harsh judge whom we can never please. Thankfully, Luther also shows us the incredible wonder of coming to know God's love for us. When we realize that God's love in Christ provides what God's holy judgment requires, it is truly as though the gates of paradise have been opened to us! We need the whole truth of Scripture: that we are spiritually ill (sinners before a holy God), *but* God provides the spiritual cure and offers us forgiveness of sin because God is love.

It's no secret that when we have mistaken beliefs about God's judgment, there are serious problems. To avoid these problems, some have downplayed God's judgment and emphasized his love. Many people today, including American church-goers and even preachers, are drawn to this option. The problem with this option, for Christians, is that God's judgment is a core part of the very gospel preached by Jesus and his apostles. The New Testament shows that God's judgment is one of the basic teachings of the faith that all Christians are expected to believe. When we neglect God's judgment, we run the risk of "making God in our own image," rather than receiving what is revealed about God in Scripture. This can have a detrimental influence on our ethics, evangelism, and theology.

An even more radical option is to believe in a God of love who is *never* wrathful in judging sin. According to the second-century leader Marcion, while the Old Testament God may have been a God of wrathful judgment, the New Testament God is a God of merciful love. Beyond the obvious heresy of teaching two different Gods, the problem with this option is that careful examination of Scripture reveals plenty of love and mercy in the Old Testament and plenty of judgment and wrath in the New Testament. Throughout the canon of Scripture, God's love and judgment are so inextricably intertwined that they cannot be torn apart. Despite the Bible's clear teaching on this subject, Marcion's view has not died, but lives on within segments of evangelicalism and the tradition of Protestant liberalism that attempts to magnify God's love while denying God's wrath. Here we see the dangers of deciding by our fallen human reason what we think God must be like, rather than receiving what God has revealed to us in the Bible.

The solution proposed in this book is for us to embrace a more full, biblical image of God—one that joins his love and judgment together. When we ponder what the world would otherwise be like, we can see that God's love and judgment are both vital divine attributes to be cherished. Over the years, theologians have suggested that God's wrath *conflicts with* God's love, that God's wrath is *subordinate to* God's love, that God's wrath is merely an *expression of* God's love, or that God's wrath and God's love must be *balanced against* one another. While there is some merit in these models, this book suggests it is better to think of God's love and wrath as expressions of his multifaceted, united character. That is, God's love and wrath both flow out of *who God is*—acting in harmony, rather than conflicting with each other. God's attributes of love and wrath are like the different facets of a brilliant diamond, which sparkle together in their beauty.

The Gospels show us that Jesus' ministry was filled with actions of love and words of judgment. As God transforms his people more and more into the image of Jesus, these two attributes should also be displayed in our relationships with others. Both godly love and godly judgment should flow out of who we are—at the right times, in the right ways, in response to the right situations. For example, God's people should reflect his image and follow Jesus' example by fusing love and judgment together when we administer godly discipline, express righteous anger, and engage in caring confrontation. Of course, God is the final judge of all things. But the last chapter shows that *love and judgment belong together not only in God but also in God's people, who bear his image.*

As we look back over this book we see that the Bible and church history teach a common message: the God of love and God of judgment are not two different "Gods" or two faces of God that are irreconcilable. Rather, love and judgment are joined together in the perfect union of God's indivisible character. To paraphrase Jesus' famous declaration on marriage, what is joined together in God (his love and judgment), let no one separate.

Bibliography

Arends, Carolyn. "The Grace of Wrath," *Christianity Today* 52 (2008) 64.

Bainton, Roland H. *Here I Stand: A Life of Martin Luther*. Nashville: Abingdon, 1950.

Barton, Bruce. *A Young Man's Jesus*. Boston: Pilgrim, 1914.

Baylor University. *The Baylor Religion Survey*. Waco, TX: Baylor Institute for Studies of Religion, 2005.

Beale, G. K. *We Become What We Worship: A Biblical Theology of Idolatry*. Downers Grove, IL: InterVarsity, 2008.

Beard, Thomas. *The Theatre of God's Judgments*. 3rd printing. London: Adam Islip, 1631.

Best, Ernest. *Ephesians: The International Critical Commentary*. Edinburgh: T & T Clark, 1998.

Brecht, Martin. *Martin Luther: His Road to Reformation, 1483–1521*. Translated by James L. Schaaf. Philadelphia: Fortress, 1985.

Bruce, F. F. *The Epistle to the Hebrews, Revised Edition*. Grand Rapids, MI: Eerdmans, 1990.

Bryan, Steven. *Jesus and Israel's Traditions of Judgment and Restoration*. New York: Cambridge University Press, 2002.

Bunyan, John. *All Loves Excelling: The Saints' Knowledge of Christ's Love*. Carlisle, PA: The Banner of Truth Trust, 1998.

Calvin, John. *Institutes of the Christian Religion*. 2 vols. Translated by Ford Lewis Battles. Edited by John T. McNeill. Philadelphia: Westminster, 1960.

Campbell, Alastair V. *The Gospel of Anger*. London: SPCK, 1986.

Carson, D. A. "The Wrath of God." In Bruce L. McCormack (ed.), *Engaging the Doctrine of God: Contemporary Protestant Perspectives*, 37–63. Grand Rapids, MI: Baker Academic, 2008.

Chambers, Sarah. "A Biblical Theology of Godly Human Anger." PhD diss., Trinity Evangelical Divinity School, 1996.

Clotfelter, David. *Sinners in the Hands of a Good God: Reconciling Divine Judgment and Mercy*. Chicago: Moody, 2004.

Danker, Frederick William Danker, editor. *A Greek-English Lexicon of the New Testament and Other Early Christian Literature*. 3rd edition. Chicago: University of Chicago Press, 2000.

Dodd, C. H. *The Apostolic Preaching and Its Development*. New York: Harper & Row, 1964.

Dungan, David L. *A History of the Synoptic Problem*. New York: Doubleday, 1999.

Dunning, John. *On the Air: The Encyclopedia of Old-Time Radio*. Oxford, England: Oxford University Press, 1998.

Ehrman, Bart. *Lost Christianities: The Battles for Scripture and the Faiths We Never Knew*. New York: Oxford University Press, 2003.

Bibliography

Erickson, Millard J. *God the Father Almighty: A Contemporary Exploration of the Divine Attributes*. Grand Rapids, MI: Baker Book House, 1998.

Evans, Norm. *On God's Squad: The Story of Norm Evans*, as told to Ray Didinger and Sonny Schwartz. Carol Stream, IL: Creation House, 1971.

Ferguson, Sinclair. *Grow in Grace*. Colorado Springs, CO: NavPress, 1984.

Fernando, Ajith. *Acts: The NIV Application Commentary*. Grand Rapids, MI: Zondervan, 1998.

Fischer, John. *12 Steps for the Recovering Pharisee (Like Me)*. Minneapolis: Bethany Publishing House, 2000.

Foster, R. A., and J. P. Keating, "Measuring Androcentrism in the Western God-Concept," *Journal for the Scientific Study of Religion* 31:3 (1992) 366–75.

France, R. T. *The Gospel According to Matthew: An Introduction and Commentary*. Leicester, England: InterVarsity, 1985.

Galli, Mark. *Jesus Mean and Wild: The Unexpected Love of an Untamable God*. Grand Rapids, MI: BakerBooks, 2006.

Grudem, Wayne. *Systematic Theology: An Introduction to Biblical Doctrine*. Grand Rapids, MI: Zondervan, 1994.

Hall, David D. *Worlds of Wonder, Days of Judgment: Popular Religious Belief in Early New England*. Cambridge, MA: Harvard University Press, 1989.

Hand, Richard J. *Terror on the Air!: Horror Radio in America, 1931–1952*. Jefferson, NC: Macfarland & Company, 2006.

Hansen, G. Walter. "The Preaching and Defence of Paul." In I. Howard Marshall and David Peterson, eds., *Witness to the Gospel: The Theology of Acts*, 295–324. Grand Rapids, MI: Eerdmans, 1998.

Hanson, Anthony T. *The Wrath of the Lamb*. London: SPCK, 1957.

Harnack, Adolf von. *Marcion: The Gospel of the Alien God*. 2nd edition. Translated by John E. Steely and Lyle D. Bierma. Durham, NC: Labyrinth, 1990.

Hindmarsh, D. Bruce. *John Newton and the Evangelical Tradition: Between the Conversions of Wesley and Wilberforce*. Oxford, England: Clarendon, 1996.

Hultgren, Arland J., and Steven A. Haggmark, editors. *The Earliest Christian Heretics: Readings from Their Opponents*. Minneapolis: Fortress, 1996.

Jefferson, Thomas. *The Philosophy of Jesus* and *The Life and Morals of Jesus*. In Dickinson W. Adams, ed. *Jefferson's Extracts from the Gospels*. Princeton, NJ: Princeton University Press, 1983.

Jonas, Hans. *The Gnostic Religion: The Message of the Alien God & the Beginnings of Christianity*. 3rd edition. Boston, MA: Beacon, 2001.

Keener, Craig S. *The IVP Bible Background Commentary: New Testament*. Downers Grove, IL: InterVarsity, 1993.

———. *Matthew*. Downers Grove, IL: InterVarsity, 1997.

Keillor, Steven J. *God's Judgments: Interpreting History and the Christian Faith*. Downer's Grove, IL: InterVarsity, 2007.

Kitamori, Kazoh. *Theology of the Pain of God*. 5th edition. Richmond, VA: John Knox, 1965.

Krejci, Mark J. "Gender Comparison of God Schemas: A Multidimensional Scaling Analysis." *The International Journal for the Psychology of Religion* 8:1 (1998) 57–66.

Kruger, C. Baxter. *Jesus and the Undoing of Adam*. Jackson, MS: Perichoresis, 2003.

Kunkel, Mark A., et. al. "God Images: A Concept Map," *Journal for the Scientific Study of Religion* 38 (1999) 193–202.

Bibliography

Lane, Tony. "The Wrath of God as an Aspect of the Love of God." In Kevin J. Vanhoozer, ed. *Nothing Greater, Nothing Better: Theological Essays on the Love of God*, 138–67. Grand Rapids, MI: Eerdmans, 2001.

Lane, William L. *Word Biblical Commentary: Hebrews 1–8*. Dallas: Word Books, 1991.

Laney, J. Carl. "God's Self-Revelation in Exodus 34:6–8," *Bibliotheca Sacra* 158 (2001) 36–51.

Larkin, William J. *Acts*. Downers Grove, IL: InterVarsity, 1995.

Lemcio, Eugene. *The Past of Jesus in the Gospels*. New York: Cambridge University Press, 1991.

Lester, Andrew D. *The Angry Christian: A Theology for Care and Counseling*. Louisville, KY: Westminster John Knox Press, 2003.

Lewis, C. S. *Reflections on the Psalms*. New York: Harcourt, Brace, and Company, 1958.

Lincoln, Andrew T. *Ephesians: Word Biblical Commentary*. Volume 42. Dallas: Word, 1990.

———. *The Gospel according to Saint John*. New York: Continuum, 2005.

Lincoln, Bruce. *Holy Terrors: Thinking about Religion after September 11*. 2nd edition. Chicago: The University of Chicago Press, 2006.

Lohse, Bernhard. *Martin Luther's Theology: Its Historical and Systematic Development*. Translated and edited by Roy A. Harrisville. Minneapolis: Fortress, 1999.

Lucado, Max. *A Love Worth Living: Living in the Overflow of God's Love*. Nashville: Thomas Nelson, 2002.

Lüdemann, Gerd. *Heretics: The Other Side of Christianity*. Translated by John Bowden. Louisville, KY: Westminster John Knox, 1996.

Luther, Martin. *D. Martin Luthers Werke: Kritische Gesamtausgabe, Abteilung Werke*. Weimar, Germany: Böhlaus, 1883-.

———. *D. Martin Luthers Werke: Kritische Gesamtausgabe, Tischreden* [Table Talk]. Weimar, Germany: Böhlaus, 1912–1921.

MacArthur, Jr., John. *God: Coming Face to Face with His Majesty*. Wheaton, IL: Victor Books, 1993.

———. *The Love of God*. Dallas: Word Publishing, 1996.

Martin, James P. *The Last Judgment in Protestant Theology from Orthodoxy to Ritschl*. Grand Rapids, MI: Eerdmans, 1963.

Martin, Sean. *The Cathars: The Most Successful Heresy of the Middle Ages*. New York: Thunder's Mouth, 2004.

Marty, Martin. *Martin Luther*. New York: Penguin Books, 2004.

Mather, Increase. *A Discourse Concerning the Uncertainty of the Times of Men* (1697). In Perry Miller and Thomas Johnson, eds. *The Puritans*, vol. 1, 340–48. New York: Harper & Row, 1963.

———. *An Essay for the Recording of Illustrious Providences*. Boston: Samuel Green, 1684. Reprinted in the Garland Library of Narratives of North American Indian Captivities, volume 2. New York: Garland, 1977.

May, Gerhard. "Marcion in Contemporary Views—Results and Open Questions," *The Second Century* 6 (1988) 129–51.

McEntyre, Marilyn Chandler. "Nice is Not the Point," *Christianity Today*, November 13 (2000) 104.

Miller, John W. "In the Footsteps of Marcion: Notes toward an Understanding of John Yoder's Theology," *Conrad Grebel Review* 16 (1998) 82–92.

Moltmann, Jürgen. *The Crucified God*. London: SCM, 1974.

Bibliography

Morgan, David. *The Lure of Images: A History of Religion and Visual Media in America.* New York: Routledge, 2007.

Moroney, Stephen K. "Higher Stages? Some Cautions for Christian Integration with Kohlberg's Theory," *Journal of Psychology and Theology* 34 (2006) 361–71.

———. *The Noetic Effects of Sin: A Historical and Contemporary Exploration of How Sin Affects Our Thinking.* Lanham, MD: Lexington Books, 2000.

Morris, Leon. *The Apostolic Preaching of the Cross.* 1st edition. Grand Rapids, MI: Eerdmans, 1955.

———. *The Biblical Doctrine of Judgment.* Grand Rapids, MI: Eerdmans, 1960.

———. "Wrath of God." In Sinclair B. Ferguson and David F. Wright (eds.), *New Dictionary of Theology,* 732. Downers Grove, IL: InterVarsity, 1988.

Nachman, Gerald. *Raised on Radio.* Berkeley, CA: University of California Press, 1998.

Newton, John. "Diary of John Newton," Unpublished: Princeton University Library.

———. *Twenty-five Letters of the Rev. John Newton.* Edinburgh: Johnstone, 1840.

———. *The Works of the Rev. John Newton . . . from the Last London Edition.* 4 vols. New Haven, CT: Nathan Whiting, 1828.

Nichols, Stephen J. *Jesus Made in America: A Cultural History from the Puritans to the Passion of the Christ.* Downers Grove, IL: InterVarsity, 2008.

———. *Martin Luther: A Guided Tour of His Life and Thought.* Philipsburg, NJ: Presbyterian and Reformed Publishing, 2002.

Niebuhr, H. Richard. *The Kingdom of God in America.* New York: Harper and Row, 1959.

Noll, Mark A. "Foreword." In Steven J. Keillor's *God's Judgments: Interpreting History and the Christian Faith.* Downer's Grove, IL: InterVarsity, 2007.

Oberman, Heiko A. *Luther: Man Between God and the Devil.* New York: Doubleday, 1992.

O'Brien, Peter. *The Letter to the Ephesians.* Grand Rapids, MI: Eerdmans, 1999.

O'Donovan, Oliver. *The Ways of Judgment: The Bampton Lectures, 2003.* Grand Rapids, MI: Eerdmans, 2005.

Olson, Roger E. *Questions to All Your Answers: The Journey from Folk Religion to Examined Faith.* Grand Rapids, MI: Zondervan, 2007.

The One Year Bible: The New International Version. Wheaton, IL: Tyndale House, 1986.

Osborn, Eric. *Tertullian, First Theologian of the West.* Cambridge, England: Cambridge University Press, 1997.

Osteen, Joel. *Become a Better You: 7 Keys to Improving Your Life Every Day.* New York: Free Press, 2007.

Packer, J. I. *Knowing God.* Downer's Grove, IL: InterVarsity, 1993.

Paulson, Steven D. "The Wrath of God," *Dialog* 33 (1994) 245–51.

Peterson, Eugene H. "Foreword." In Mark Galli, *Jesus Mean and Wild: The Unexpected Love of an Untamable God.* Grand Rapids, MI: BakerBooks, 2006.

Phipps, William E. *Amazing Grace in John Newton: Slave-Ship Captain, Hymnwriter, and Abolitionist.* Macon, GA: Mercer University Press, 2001.

Pink, Arthur W. *The Attributes of God.* Grand Rapids, MI: Baker Books, 2006.

Pinnock, Clark H. and Brow, Robert C. *Unbounded Love: A Good News Theology for the 21st Century.* Downers Grove, IL: InterVarsity, 1994.

Raabe, Paul R. "The Two 'Faces' of Yahweh: Divine Wrath and Mercy in the Old Testament." In Gerald S. Krispin and Jon D. Vieker (eds.). *And Every Tongue Confess,* 283–310. Chelsea, MI: BookCrafters, 1990.

Reiser, Marius. *Jesus and Judgment.* Minneapolis: Fortress, 1997.

Bibliography

Ritschl, Albrect. *The Christian Doctrine of Justification and Reconciliation.* H. R. Mackintosh and A. B. Macaulay (trans. and ed.). Clifton, NJ: Reference Book Publishers, 1966.

Roof, Wade Clark and Roof, Jennifer L. "Review of the Polls: Images of God among Americans," *Journal for the Scientific Study of Religion* 23 (1984) 201–5.

Schleiermacher, Friedrich. *The Christian Faith.* H. R. Mackintosh and J. S. Stewart (eds.). New York: Harper & Row, 1963.

———. *The Life of Jesus.* Jack C. Verheyden (ed.) and S. Maclean Gilmour (trans.). Philadelphia: Fortress, 1975.

———. "The Wrath of God." In Dawn DeVries (trans. and ed.), *Servant of the Word: Selected Sermons of Friedrich Schleiermacher.* Philadelphia: Fortress, 1987.

Schnackenburg, Rudolf. *Ephesians: A Commentary.* Translated by Helen Heron. Edinburgh: T & T Clark, 1991.

Smith, Christian and Denton, Melinda Lundquist. *Soul Searching: The Religious and Spiritual Lives of American Teenagers.* New York: Oxford University Press, 2005.

Snodgrass, Klyne. *Ephesians: The NIV Application Commentary.* Grand Rapids, MI: Zondervan, 1996.

———. "Justification by Grace—to the Doers: An Analysis of the Place of Romans 2 in the Theology of Paul," *New Testament Studies* 32 (1986) 72–93.

Snyderman, Nancy L. *Medical Myths That Can Kill You: And the 101 Truths That Will Save, Extend, and Improve Your Life.* New York: Crown, 2008.

Spieckermann, Hermann. "God's Steadfast Love: Towards a New Conception of Old Testament Theology," *Biblica* 81 (2000) 305–27.

Spong, John Shelby. *The Sins of Scripture: Exposing the Bible's Texts of Hate to Reveal the God of Love.* San Francisco: HarperSanFrancisco, 2005.

———. *Why Christianity Must Change or Die: A Bishop Speaks to Believers in Exile.* San Francisco: HarperSanFrancisco, 1998.

Sproul, R. C. *The Character of God: Discovering the God Who Is.* Ann Arbor, MI: Vine, 1995.

———. *The Consequences of Ideas: Understanding the Concepts That Shaped Our World.* Wheaton, IL: Crossway, 2000.

Steinmetz, David C. *Luther in Context.* 2nd edition. Grand Rapids, MI: Baker, 2002.

Stott, John R. W. *God's New Society: The Message of Ephesians.* Downers Grove, IL: InterVarsity, 1979.

———. *The Letters of John: An Introduction and Commentary.* Leicester, England: InterVarsity, 1994.

———. *Romans: God's Good News for the World.* Downers Grove, IL: InterVarsity, 1994.

Stoyanov, Yuri. *The Other God: Dualist Religions from Antiquity to the Cathar Heresy.* New Haven: Yale University Press, 2000.

Tasker, R. V. G. *The Biblical Doctrine of the Wrath of God.* London: Tyndale, 1951.

Thomas, Paul W. "Judgment," *The Expository Times* 105 (1994) 106–10.

Tipson, Baird. "Invisible Saints: The 'Judgment of Charity' in the Early New England Churches," *Church History* 44 (1975) 460–71.

Tozer, A. W. *The Knowledge of the Holy.* New York: Harper, 1961.

Travis, Stephen H. *Christ and the Judgement of God: The Limits of Divine Retribution in New Testament Thought.* 2nd edition. Peabody, MA: Hendrickson, 2009.

Trueman, Carl. "The Marcions Have Landed!" *Themelios* 28 (2002) 1–4.

Tucker, Ruth A. *God Talk: Cautions for Those Who Hear God's Voice.* Downer's Grove, IL: InterVarsity, 2005.

Bibliography

Van Der Lans, Jan. "Empirical Research into the Human Images of God: A Review and Some Considerations." In Hans-Georg Ziebertz, Friedrich Schweitzer, Hermann Haring, and Don Browning (eds.), *The Human Image of God*. Leiden: Brill, 2001.

VanderMolen, Ronald J. "Providence as Mystery, Providence as Revelation: Puritan and Anglican Modifications of John Calvin's Doctrine of Providence," *Church History* 47 (1978) 27–47.

VanLandingham, Chris. *Judgment & Justification in Early Judaism and the Apostle Paul*. Peabody, MA: Hendrickson, 2006.

Via, Dan O. *Divine Justice, Divine Judgment*. Minneapolis: Fortress, 2007.

Walsham, Alexandra. *Providence in Early Modern England*. New York: Oxford University Press, 1999.

Walter, Tony. *The Eclipse of Eternity: A Sociology of the Afterlife*. New York: St. Martin's, 1996.

Weaver, Richard M. *Ideas Have Consequences*. Chicago: University of Chicago Press, 1948.

Whitacre, Rodney A. *John*. Downers Grove, IL: InterVarsity, 1999.

Witherington III, Ben. *The Acts of the Apostles: A Socio-Rhetorical Commentary*. Grand Rapids, MI: Eerdmans, 1998.

Wright, Christopher J. H. *The God I Don't Understand: Reflections on Tough Questions of Faith*. Grand Rapids, MI: Zondervan, 2008.

Yancey, Philip. *Church: Why Bother? My Personal Pilgrimage*. Grand Rapids, MI: Zondervan, 1998.

———. *The Jesus I Never Knew*. Grand Rapids, MI: Zondervan, 1995.

Yinger, Kent L. *Paul, Judaism, and Judgment According to Deeds*. Cambridge, England: Cambridge University Press, 1999.

Zachman, Randall C. "The Unity of Judgment and Love," *Ex Auditu* 20 (2004) 148–61.

Ziebertz, Hans-Georg, editor. *Imagining God: Empirical Explorations from an International Perspective*. Münster: Lit Verlag, 2001.